THE POLITICS OF
PUERTO RICAN UNIVERSITY STUDENTS

Latin American Monographs, No. 20
Institute of Latin American Studies
The University of Texas at Austin

The POLITICS of PUERTO RICAN UNIVERSITY STUDENTS

ARTHUR LIEBMAN

Published for the
INSTITUTE OF LATIN AMERICAN STUDIES
BY THE UNIVERSITY OF TEXAS PRESS, AUSTIN AND LONDON

International Standard Book Number 0-292-70046-6
Library of Congress Catalog Card Number 78-630381
Copyright © 1970 by Arthur Liebman
All rights reserved
Manufactured in the United States of America

220991

To my wife, Edna
To my parents, Mr. & Mrs. Sol Liebman
To my graduate dean, Dean Sanford S. Elberg

ACKNOWLEDGMENTS

This study is part of the Comparative Universities Project sponsored jointly by the Brookings Institute and the Center for International Affairs, Harvard University, and was supported by grants from the Ford Foundation, the Carnegie Corporation, and the National Institute of Mental Health. My principal source of professional assistance was Seymour Martin Lipset, Director of the Comparative Universities Project. Professors Nathan Glazer and Joseph Fischer also took time from their busy schedules to wade through this manuscript and to improve it through their suggestions and criticisms.

My stay and my research in Puerto Rico were made both pleasant and meaningful by countless Puerto Ricans. One who proved most hospitable as well as informative was Professor Robert Anderson, the Chairman of the Political Science Department and now Dean of the School of Social Sciences of the University of Puerto. I am also grateful to the students, faculty, and administrators of the university who gave of their time and thoughts to yet another visiting social scientist from the United States. I would especially like to thank the members of FUPI for their cooperation.

Finally, I would like to acknowledge a huge debt to two people, my wife, Edna, and Dean Sanford S. Elberg of the Graduate Division of the University of California. Dean Elberg demonstrated that an administrator of a multiversity can at the same time be a warm and understanding human being. Through his faith in me I was able to complete both this study and my graduate career. The least of the many kind things that he did for me was to render financial assistance.

To my wife, who throughout the course of the study was a major source of inspiration and help, I acknowledge a debt that will take me the rest of my life to repay. Without her faith and her nudging, I seriously doubt whether I would have finished.

CONTENTS

THE POLITICS OF
PUERTO RICAN UNIVERSITY STUDENTS

Chapter I

INTRODUCTION

The central concern of this study is the political attitudes and activities of Puerto Rican university students. The distinguishing characteristic of the student body at the University of Puerto Rico is the lack of a strong leftist-nationalist movement. Contrary to the popular impression of the Latin American student as a radical nationalist, the Puerto Rican student tends to be satisfied with the status quo and looks forward to the time when he will share in the benefits of his acquisitive society. Although one would expect these students, a select minority of their age cohort and a part of a unique subculture, to differ from the general populace, these students are also the children of their fathers. University students in Puerto Rico and elsewhere do not exist in a void. They are members of a society who have been socialized to the values, norms, and traditions of that society. Their political behavior is conducted within the context of existing social, economic, and political conditions. The act of entering a university does not liberate the student from familial and societal ties. As Kalman Silvert states: "The Latin American student is the child of his parents. To assume that the student is but a hoteyed revolutionary is to presume that somehow registering in a university is sufficient to cut family ties, break class and other group identifications, and produce a special kind of creature divorced from his society."[1] It therefore seems necessary to

[1] Kalman H. Silvert, "The University Student," in *Continuity and Change in Latin America*, ed. John Johnson, p. 225. Studies of student and adolescent politics in the United States reveal that in terms of political inheritance American students also tend to be children of their fathers. However, one generally

discover the nature of the societal and cultural influences working upon the student in order to better understand his politics.

A consideration of the politics of university students in Puerto Rico or, for that matter, of any Puerto Rican group, must take into account the issue of the island's political status. In Puerto Rican history as well as in the present, the status issue is the focus of political concerns. "In fact, it is this 'status' issue that is generally considered to be *the* political issue on the island; other problems are often referred to as 'administrative' or 'technical' problems."[2] For over one hundred years whether a Puerto Rican is politically left, right, or center has been gauged solely by his position regarding the status of the relationship between Puerto Rico and the metropolitan power.

THE SIGNIFICANCE OF HISTORY

The history of the relationship between Puerto Rico and Spain, as well as that between Puerto Rico and the United States, provides insight into the historical factors that have shaped present-day Puerto Rican politics. No people are ever able to free themselves completely from their history and traditions. As Marx said in *The Eighteenth Brumaire of Louis Bonaparte*, "Men make their own history, but they do not make it under circumstances chosen by themselves, but under circumstances directly found, given and transmitted from the past." One major fact of Puerto Rican history, which no doubt bears heavily upon the present generation, is the absence of a major movement dedicated to the fight for Puerto Rican independence. For 390 years Puerto Rico stood alone among the Spanish colonies, dubiously distinguished by never having risen in arms against her mother country. The one exception to this

---

does not think of Latin American students in these terms because of the seemingly disproportionate number of radical activists among the young. See the discussion in Chapter III concerning influence of family and pertinent references.

[2] Robert Anderson, *Party Politics in Puerto Rico*, p. 12.

general rule occurred in 1868, when a brief revolt took place in the mountain town of Lares. The response of the Puerto Rican people and their leaders to this minor uprising has been characterized as "an eloquent apathy."[3] From the first quarter of the nineteenth century, when the Spanish colonies in South America lifted the banner of revolt, until the Cubans fought fiercely for their independence from 1868 to 1895, Spanish troops had little difficulty in Puerto Rico. In fact, the island served as a military base from which Spain tried to quell the independence of her more restive colonies. Puerto Rico's transfer from Spain to the United States, a consequence of the Spanish-American War, caused no change in her political behavior, and the island's record of nonrevolutionary activity has remained virtually unblemished. Under both Spain and the United States, the distinguishing characteristics of Puerto Rican politics have been "passivity, pragmatism, and patience."[4] One Puerto Rican official recently described Puerto Rico in the following manner: "We'd get all sorts of attention if a bunch of us decided to start fighting and yelling and demonstrating and picketing against U.S. colonialism. But that's simply not the way most of us are used to being. We're essentially a peaceful people, we always have been, who believe in legislation, law and order."[5]

Puerto Ricans can commemorate no glorious political or military successes and, with the minor exception of Lares, can point to no heroic defeats. What has been said of Australia can be equally applied to Puerto Rico: ". . . in the traditional experience of Australia there were no events which fired the imagination and uplifted the heart. There was no glorious past to which Australian sons would wish to recur in memory and legend."[6] Consequently present-day nationalists, student or adult, are somewhat handi-

[3] *Ibid.*, p. 4.
[4] *Ibid.*, p. 5.
[5] Kal Wagenheim, "Puerto Rico: Kinship or Colony," *New Leader*, 49 (May 23, 1966), 11.
[6] Richard N. Rosencrance, "The Radical Culture of Australia," in *The Founding of New Societies*, ed. Louis Hartz, p. 29.

capped. Their appeals for independence from the United States cannot be couched in historical terms capable of arousing great emotion. In fact, the opposite is true; militant support for independence places the proponent outside the mainstream of Puerto Rican tradition. The nationalist has little that he can call forth from Puerto Rican history to legitimize his position. Whenever violence has been associated with the cause of independence, as in the assassination of the chief of police by Nationalist gunmen in 1936 or in the abortive Nationalist revolt in 1950, the effect has been a loss of popular support for the political group involved.[7]

The lack of direct action for independence against the Spanish has had its counterpart at the ballot box under United States rule. In 1932 the Nationalist party, dedicated to the freedom of Puerto Rico by any means, received less than 2 percent of the votes cast in the election. It never returned to the ballot. The only other political party committed to Puerto Rican independence to appear on the ballot has been the Partido Independentista Puertorriqueño (PIP). In 1948, its first time on the ballot, the PIP polled 10 percent of all the votes. In the next election, in 1952, its support almost doubled with 19 percent of the votes. To date, this has been its highpoint. In the last two elections, the PIP percentage of the votes has hovered around 3 percent.[8]

Why has Puerto Rico successfully resisted the appeals of nationalism, especially when at various times in the nineteenth and twentieth centuries nationalism has swept through so many areas of the world? To answer this question, one must focus upon the contributing historical and structural factors. The underlying assumption of this endeavor is that those factors that have restricted the development and support of nationalism among the Puerto Rican populace play a large role in determining the political behavior of Puerto Rican university students.

---

[7] Gordon K. Lewis, *Puerto Rico: Freedom and Power in the Caribbean*, pp. 135–136; Anderson, *Party Politics*, p. 45.

[8] *Ibid.*, pp. 43, 232.

The Weakness of Indigenous Institutions[9]

"The main genius of Hispanic colonization tended to bypass Borinquén [Puerto Rico]."[10] There was little in the small and resource-poor island of Puerto Rico to attract the attention of colonists or fortune hunters. Because of its strategic position, however, Puerto Rico served the Spanish Empire as a military bastion. Under the Spanish rule the *situado*, an annual sum paid from the viceroyalty of Mexico for salaries and expenses of the military garrison, was a major part of the island's revenues. Into the nineteenth century military officers appointed by the Spanish homeland ruled Puerto Rico. The local populace had no influence either in the choice of their rulers or in the policy decisions made by those men. "The governor was accountable only to the *Ministerio del Ultramar* in Madrid; he alone appointed the members of his council; and in his fourfold capacity as captain general of the local military and naval forces, as *Intendente*, as superior judge in the judicial system, and as *Vicepatrón* in all religious matters, he exercised complete local authority over all aspects of the national life; and remained, in effect, the unilateral source of all official authority."[11]

Throughout the Spanish rule, communication within the island of Puerto Rico was difficult. From earliest days the peasants, or *jíbaros*, of an already predominantly rural population preferred to settle apart from each other.[12] Not only did this dispersal hamper communication within rural areas, but the scarcity of adequate roads and railroads impeded communication between rural and

---

[9] Major sources upon which this section draws are Lewis, *Freedom and Power*, pp. 47–67; Anderson, *Party Politics*, pp. 1–6; Richard M. Morse, "La transformación ilusoria de Puerto Rico," *Revista de Ciencias Sociales*, 4, no. 2 (June, 1960), 357–376; V. S. Clark, *Porto Rico and Its Problems*, pp. 540–548; J. H. Steward *et al.*, "The Cultural Background of Contemporary Puerto Rico," in *The People of Puerto Rico*, ed. J. H. Steward *et al.*, pp. 29–90.

[10] Lewis, *Freedom and Power*, p. 47.

[11] *Ibid.*, p. 50.

[12] José C. Rosario, "The Porto Rican and His Historical Antecedents," in Clark, *Porto Rico and Its Problems*, pp. 540–545.

urban areas as well.[13] The first American Commissioner to Puerto Rico, Henry K. Carroll, reported to President McKinley that the most frequent request he received was for roads.[14] As one Puerto Rican official testifying before Commissioner Carroll in 1899 expressed it, "Real roads do not exist from the interior to the coast; only tracks, dangerous even to travelers."[15] Another claimed, "After four centuries of existence we are almost cut off from intercommunication. Of our internal roads, it is best to say nothing; no one dares journey by them."[16] The first railroad in Puerto Rico was not built until 1880. When the Americans landed in 1898 there were only 272 miles of unconnected rail lines with no uniform width of gauge.[17]

Spanish mercantile policy inhibited the natural development and growth of the Puerto Rican economy. Puerto Rican sugar and other products were denied free entry into the Spanish market, and trading with such neighboring areas as the United States was prohibited. The Spanish also curtailed the establishment of any industry in Puerto Rico that might compete with industry in the mother country. When the Americans assumed control, they found only a few small industries.[18]

The development of a native Puerto Rican middle and upper class was also hampered by Spanish domination of the island. "The commerce of Puerto Rico was controlled almost entirely by Spanish and European houses. Comparatively few Puerto Ricans were engaged in either the banking or the mercantile branch. The leading retail merchants were also Spaniards and had Spanish clerks."[19] The chief governmental positions were in Spanish hands.[20] In

---

[13] Arturo Morales-Carrión, *Puerto Rico and the Non-Hispanic Caribbean: A Study in the Decline of Spanish Exclusivism*, pp. 58, 85.

[14] Henry K. Carroll, *Report on the Island of Porto Rico*, p. 38.

[15] *Ibid.*

[16] *Ibid.*, p. 159.

[17] *Ibid.*, pp. 38, 164.

[18] Rosario, "Historical Antecedents," pp. 542–546; Thomas D. Curtis, *Land Reform, Democracy, and Economic Interest in Puerto Rico*, pp. 3–8.

[19] Carroll, *Island of Porto Rico*, p. 42.

[20] Rosario, "Historical Antecedents," p. 545.

1877 even Puerto Rican teachers were ordered replaced by Spanish women or Spanish soldiers stationed on the island.[21] With the exception of Puerto Rican planters, some of whom were able to amass large incomes, few Puerto Ricans held positions of importance.

Internally, Puerto Rico developed no social, economic, or cultural institutions that might have served to mold a Puerto Rican identity. According to Glazer and Moynihan in *Beyond the Melting Pot*, Puerto Rico lacked "the net of culture [that] keeps up pride and encourages effort."[22] The hacienda system of landholdings common in other parts of Spanish America was not prevalent in Puerto Rico. San Juan, the major city on the island, provided no focus of intellectual or aristocratic activity. Catholicism was the only recognized and permitted religion on the island, but the Church never made extensive inroads into rural areas and had only a weak hold on the populace in general. The poverty of the Church, the great shortage of priests, and the Church's inability, under both Spanish and American rule, to recruit a native-born clergy contributed to the failure of the Catholic church to establish itself as a strong indigenous institution. Consequently, when American superseded Spanish rule, the Puerto Ricans, unlike the Polish and the Irish in the United States, could not effectively associate support for the Church with maintenance of a national identity.

No university appeared in Puerto Rico during the time of Spanish control; the first university was built and financed by the Americans in 1903. Absence of a university deprived Puerto Rico of the native-born and nationally conscious intelligentsia necessary for intellectual tradition to buttress national consciousness.

Some Puerto Ricans did gain access to higher education. Most received this education in Spain. Others attended universities in Santo Domingo, Caracas, Havana, and the United States. Political factors prevented more widespread use of educational institutions near the island. In fact, youth and their families were actively discouraged from looking toward the United States for university

[21] Carroll, *Island of Porto Rico*, pp. 42, 621.
[22] Nathan Glazer and Daniel P. Moynihan, *Beyond the Melting Pot: The Ethnic Groups of New York City*, p. 88.

education. Education in the United States, authorities felt, would corrupt and subvert Puerto Rican students: Those who did study in the United States were accused of harboring radical ideas.[23]

However, a Spanish education did not orient Puerto Rican students to the problems of their native island. A Latin American sociologist has pointed out that Latin Americans who attended local schools remained more "provincial" and Latin American in their outlook than did their counterparts who had studied in France and Spain, who looked upon themselves as cosmopolitans.[24] Furthermore, Puerto Ricans educated in Europe came from a class that thought of itself as Spanish to begin with, not Puerto Rican.[25] Although many students returning from their studies abroad did become liberal and progressive toward the political, social, and intellectual problems of Puerto Rico, the absence of a university in Puerto Rico inhibited the formation of disparate individuals into a circle, club, or school of thought concerned with the island's problems.[26]

The absence of a university has made the cultural heritage of Puerto Rico difficult to preserve. Contemporary historians examining the sixteenth, seventeenth, and eighteenth centuries have complained of the lack of adequate sources. Puerto Rican histories and historical texts used in the schools today deal predominantly with the latter part of the nineteenth century. Consequently, to the extent that a nationalist movement requires a firm historical base and a populace capable of identifying with its own past, Puerto Rican nationalism is and has been virtually impotent.

The failure to establish a significant nationalist movement in

[23] Lewis, *Freedom and Power*, pp. 441–442; "*San Juan Review* Interviews the Secretary of Education," *San Juan Review*, 2, no. 5 (June, 1965), 13–16; Columbia University, Teachers College, *A Survey of the Public Educational System of Puerto Rico*, p. 27.

[24] Juan José Osuna, *A History of Education in Puerto Rico*, p. 94.

[25] José Medina Echavarría, "A Sociologist's View," in *Social Aspects of Development in Latin America*, vol. 2, ed. José Medina Echavarría and Benjamin Higgins, pp. 46–48.

[26] R. H. Scheele, "The Prominent Families of Puerto Rico," in *People of Puerto Rico*, ed. Steward *et al.*, pp. 418–440.

Puerto Rico under Spanish rule can also be attributed, in part, to the expulsion of Spain from the South American continent. The success of the independence movements in Latin America contributed to the isolation of Puerto Rico and hindered the development of a Puerto Rican national identity. Spain's defeat led her to concentrate her energies on Puerto Rico and Cuba. Determined to hold on to these two last vestiges of a great empire, Spain attempted to insulate these possessions as much as possible from subversive influences from both North and South America. In addition, Puerto Rico served as a haven for the defeated Latin American loyalists, much as Canada provided refuge to the American Tories (and much as present-day Puerto Rico shelters anti-Castro Cubans). These exiles tended to be very conservative in their values as well as in their politics.[27] Intensely loyal to the Spanish motherland, these loyalist refugees, who gained an influential position on the island, were naturally hostile to any movement in Puerto Rico that promoted reform or relaxation of Spanish control.

Puerto Rico remained a small, poor backwater of the Spanish empire. Under Spanish rule, Puerto Ricans were kept relatively isolated and dependent upon Spain. Few Spanish institutions were transplanted onto Puerto Rican soil, and strong indigenous institutions did not emerge. As a result, Puerto Ricans lacked the bases upon which they might have established a major nationalist movement.

The Impact of the United States

Puerto Rico passed from Spanish to American rule as a result of the victory of the United States in the Spanish-American War in 1898. Few Puerto Ricans regretted the departure of Spain, and most looked forward to life under the American reign. The United States was generally regarded as a wealthy, dynamic, and liberal country that would bring many benefits to the Puerto Rican people.

---

[27] Carroll, *Island of Porto Rico*, p. 14; Edward J. Berbusse, S. J., *The United States in Puerto Rico, 1898–1900*, p. 9.

Since 1898, Puerto Rican attitudes toward the United States have vacillated among friendship, animosity, and ambivalence, as the impact of the American presence has spread through all segments of the society. Nonetheless, American influence has shaped the boundaries within which Puerto Ricans conduct their politics, particularly in the cultural and economic spheres.

One of the first projects launched by the Americans was the expansion and the transformation of the educational system in Puerto Rico. In 1898 about 85 percent of the population on the island was illiterate, and about 92 percent of the children between the ages of five and seventeen were not attending school. Money was poured into education and numerous schools were built. The number of students in the school system rose from a low of 44,681 students in 1898 to 176,000 in 1920. The number of teachers grew from 632 in 1900 to 14,000 in 1960.[28]

The United States not only promoted the development of education but also made certain policy decisions regarding the Puerto Rican educational system. One such decision dealt with the alternatives of emphasis upon the elementary system or emphasis upon higher education. Contrary to the desires of the island's elite, the American commissioners of education decided to extend as well as to expand elementary school education before concentrating on university education. This policy decision was one of the earlier indications that the Americans were going to build an educational system modeled after that of the mainland rather than after the elitist systems of Europe and Latin America.

However, the Americans did recognize the need for a Puerto Rican university. The University of Puerto Rico came into being in 1903. The university that emerged under the American plan differed from those of other parts of Latin America as well as from those of Europe. It stressed practical training rather than the arts and letters. A law dealing with the university established the following priorities: (1) teacher training, (2) agricultural and mechanical training, (3) natural sciences and engineering, (4) liberal

---

[28] Osuna, *History of Education*, pp. 93–112.

arts, (5) medicine, (6) law, and (7) pharmacy.[29] But the wealthier elements of Puerto Rican society "wanted a university patterned after the classical Spanish type—emphasis on arts and letters and none on science."[30] When the American view prevailed, the upper classes virtually boycotted the University of Puerto Rico. As late as 1947 a study of two hundred prominent Puerto Rican families estimated that 90 percent of the sons and almost 50 percent of the daughters of these families attended college outside the island, primarily in the United States.[31] There are also indications that the children of the elite relative to other groups in the Puerto Rican society are still sent outside Puerto Rico for their university educations. Gordon Lewis, a professor at the University of Puerto Rico and author of a major work on Puerto Rico, claimed in private conversation that the Puerto Rican intellectual and social elite generally attend such universities in the United States as the University of Chicago, Columbia University, and Harvard University. Few attend schools in Spain, and virtually none go to universities in Latin America. To date, the University of Puerto Rico has remained an open rather than elitist university, with emphasis still upon such practical areas as business and education, as opposed to such liberal arts areas as humanities and law. (The practical orientation of the University of Puerto Rico, depriving the student body of members from the upper class, has also had consequences for the development of the left that are discussed later.)

The policies that have caused the most antagonism, however, are those dealing with Americanization and the language issue. From the beginning, the new rulers looked upon the educational system as a means of merging the Puerto Rican and American social structures. One of the specific ways this was to be accomplished was through the learning of English. As the Teachers College (Columbia University) *Survey of the Public Educational System of Porto Rico* states: "Political, social, and economic expediency makes it desirable that large numbers of Puerto Ricans,

[29] *Ibid.*, p. 250.
[30] Vincenzo Petrullo, *Puerto Rican Paradox*, p. 50.
[31] Scheele, "Prominent Families of Puerto Rico," p. 440.

ultimately all of them, should be given a thorough knowledge of English. Thus they will become in time thoroughly merged into the social structure of the great Republic, with all its social and economic advantages."[32] In accord with this policy, English was established as the sole language of instruction in all grades in 1898. From 1900 on, however, this policy fluctuated, and it was not until 1948 that any firm and consistent policy was put into effect. In 1948, for the first time since 1898, Spanish was established as the only language of instruction for all grade levels. English was designated as a preferred subject until recently; it now ranks equally among other principal subjects of the curriculum.[33]

Many of the better private schools, including the parochial ones, continue to use English as the primary medium of instruction. At the university many of the texts are written in English, and instructors in such fields as medicine, biology, and natural sciences lecture in English. Although Spanish is the official medium of instruction in the Puerto Rican school system, most Puerto Ricans concerned with social mobility for themselves or for their children realize that a good command of English is a *sine qua non* for success both at the university and in the occupational world.

The abolition of English as a language of instruction in the public schools of Puerto Rico did not presage the end of the American influence upon Puerto Rican education. American educators, particularly those from Teachers College, Columbia University, are regularly consulted on aspects of the Puerto Rican educational system, and their suggestions often carry great weight. Until 1961 two of the seven members of the Superior Educational Council, the governing board of the University of Puerto Rico, were continental Americans. Many Puerto Rican educators, administrators, and teachers come to the United States to take courses, to participate in seminars, and to consult with their American counterparts. Most of the texts used in both private and public schools throughout the island are American ones translated into Spanish. Even the basic

---

[32] Columbia University, Teachers College, *Public Educational System*, p. 30.
[33] Adrian Hull, "The English Problem," *San Juan Review*, 2, no. 5 (June, 1965), 30–31.

college text that reports the history of the island was written by an American.

The educational system of Puerto Rico from elementary to university levels came under Puerto Rican control in 1948, when the first elected governor of the island appointed his commissioner of education. Puerto Rican political control brought about the change in the language policy mentioned earlier. In other areas, however, the major portion of the material taught in the classrooms remains similar to that presented during the pre-1948 period of formal control by the United States. Students, regardless of their educational level, are rarely exposed to the history of Puerto Rico in the public or private schools. At the elementary level, there is not one course devoted to the history of Puerto Rico. During four years of high school, the only formal knowledge of Puerto Rican history is learned from a one-semester course. At the University of Puerto Rico, only students in the Schools of Humanities and Social Sciences and some in the School of Education are taught Puerto Rican history. The extent of their exposure is limited to the one two-semester course offered by the Department of History.

The American influence in the cultural sphere extends beyond the educational system. The mass media in Puerto Rico are predominantly American in orientation and in content. Much of what appears on television and movie screens throughout the island originates in the United States. Advertisements and commercials for goods sold in Puerto Rico are identical to those used on the mainland. Magazines and books sold in the stands and stores throughout the island are invariably American. The news, other than that of the island, is derived primarily from dispatches of the Associated Press, the United Press, and the *New York Times*, and from radio and television networks on the mainland. Imported American holidays, such as Mother's Day, Father's Day, and the Fourth of July, are widely celebrated in Puerto Rico. Among the heroes of the Puerto Rican school children are such men as George Washington and Franklin Roosevelt. Conversely, Don Pedro Albizu Campos, the Nationalist leader who during the height of his popularity counted among his numerous followers Señora

Muñoz Marín, the wife of the former governor and leader of the Popular Democratic party, as well as Chancellor Jaime Benítez, is never mentioned in Puerto Rican schools and popular media.

As noticeable as the American impact upon the Puerto Rican culture is the absence of Latin American influence. Little is taught about Latin America or the Caribbean in the Puerto Rican schools. The mass media's coverage of the Latin American scene is as extensive and consistent as that of the coverage by the mainland's media, which means, in effect, that coverage of Latin America is neither extensive nor consistent. Another indicator of the disparity between Latin American and North American influence in Puerto Rico is the cost and the frequency of travel from Puerto Rico to the United States and from Puerto Rico to Latin America. Puerto Ricans pay less to fly to New York City than to Mexico or Venezuela, which are nearer to the island. Planes between the mainland and Puerto Rico fly on an hourly basis, but planes between Latin America and the island are available on only two or three days of the week. Although Puerto Rican cultural and political leaders speak of Puerto Rico's role as a bridge between the North American and Latin American cultures, the traffic has been restricted, for the most part, to the span between Puerto Rico and the United States.

After more than half a century of United States' predominance on the island, Puerto Ricans tend to look at the world and themselves from an American perspective. The United States has been quite successful in legitimizing its position in Puerto Rico in a way that transcends the political meaning of the term. American norms and values have been internalized.[34] This has led to the establishment of a cultural hierarchy with American values at the top and Latin American and Puerto Rican ones at the bottom. To be fash-

[34] A similar phenomenon has often been noted among Negroes in the United States in their relationships with whites. See Lewis, *Freedom and Power*, pp. 291–317. Manuel Maldonado Denis, "Política y cultura puertorriqueña," *Revista de Ciencias Sociales*, 7, nos. 1 and 2 (March and June, 1963), 141–148; René Marqués, "El puertorriqueña docil," *Revista de Ciencias Sociales*, 7, nos. 1 and 2 (March and June, 1963), 35–78.

ionable, to be modern, and to be socially successful is to be as American as possible. This includes striving to purchase American goods from cars and televisions to bottles of Coca Cola.[35] Fashionable and exclusive clubs have appeared on the island that resemble their American counterparts even to denying admission to darker-skinned Puerto Ricans. Fluency in English is as much a requirement for social acceptability at the higher levels as it is for economic mobility.[36]

The Puerto Ricans' political attitudes also seem to be influenced by American attitudes and perspectives. Although the Communist party in Puerto Rico is virtually nonexistent, the internal danger of communism is constantly raised as an issue by the mass media and politicians. The Communist label is attached to many activities and persons. Student disturbances are immediately labeled as Communist. Proindependence supporters are regarded as Communists. Any manifestation of anti-Americanism is identified as Communist inspired.[37]

The Cuban exile community, in particular, is very concerned about the Communist menace. Their influence extends beyond their numbers, as many occupy middle-class positions and some hold important jobs in the mass media. In fact, one of the most popular magazines on the island, *Bohemia*, is Cuban controlled, virulently anti-Communist, and, of course, anti-Castro. These

35 In 1965 a Puerto Rican government agency hired an advertising agency to improve the image of the goods that were made on the island. Too much money, the government felt, was being spent on the purchase of goods simply because they were made on the mainland, although cheaper island-made equivalents were readily available. Puerto Rican goods had such a negative image that Puerto Rican manufacturers gave English names to their products *(San Juan Review*, 2, no. 6 [July, 1965], 38).

36 Puerto Rican supervisory personnel employed by American firms are often chosen primarily upon their ability to speak English. "As a result, persons with superior abilities are bypassed in favor of those who know English but may be mediocre in other respects" (Lloyd G. Reynolds and Peter Gregory, *Wages, Productivity, and Industrialization in Puerto Rico*, p. 124).

37 There is a joke in Puerto Rico concerning the nature of the internal Communist menace. One Puerto Rican, attempting to assure another about the local Communists, claimed, "There are at most a dozen Communists on the island." The other replied, "Yes, but they are all on the governor's staff."

exiles, like their nineteenth-century counterparts, also strongly oppose any leftist-liberal movement, especially one that advocates independence for Puerto Rico.

Gazing beyond their island, Puerto Ricans interpret events in American terms. With one or two notable exceptions, the American intervention in the Dominican Republic was generally applauded by the mass media. Recently, the island's legislature endorsed American policy in Vietnam with but one dissenting vote cast. There is a tendency to contrast Puerto Rico's economic and political security with that of other areas in Latin America. Many come to the conclusion, with the aid of politicians and the media, that Puerto Rico owes its security to its association with the United States.

In sum, the American cultural impact upon the Puerto Rican people has been considerable. It is difficult for anyone in Puerto Rico, particularly the urban dweller, to engage in any social behavior or to entertain meaningful attitudes and opinions outside the American system of values and norms. Puerto Ricans, including students, shoppers at Sears and Woolworth's, voters, government employees, and Puerto Rican employees in American-owned enterprises, are confronted daily with American advertisements, beliefs, practices, and values. Under these conditions, maintaining a positively evaluated Puerto Rican identity becomes increasingly difficult.[38]

THE PUERTO RICAN ECONOMY

The Puerto Rican economy is characterized by economic growth, as well as by the domination of United States' interests. If we take 1940 as the base year, when Luis Muñoz Marín and the Popular Democratic party came into power, there can be no question that

---

[38] Major sources upon which this section draws are Lewis, *Freedom and Power*, pp. 291–317. Denis, "Política y cultura puertorriqueña," pp. 141–148; Petrullo, "English Problem," pp. 130–146. Marques, "El puertorriqueño dócil," pp. 35–78; *San Juan Star*, May–July, 1965; *El Mundo*, May–July, 1965; *El Imparcial*, May–July, 1965; observations and interviews conducted during the summer of 1965.

since then great changes have occurred in the Puerto Rican economy. The gross national product has risen from $288 million to $2,232 million in 1963. During this same period per capita income rose from $118 to $740. Hourly wages in manufacturing jumped from 19¢ to $1.09 per hour.

Until World War II, Puerto Rico was a predominantly agrarian society; since then it has become increasingly industrial. In 1940, 44.7 percent of the labor force was employed in agriculture, compared to 10.9 percent in manufacturing. By 1962 the percentage of agricultural workers had declined to 23.6 percent, while the percentage of industrial workers had grown to 15.6 percent. This shift toward industrialization can also be seen in the growing numbers employed in commerce and government. From 1940 to 1963 the number of government workers increased from 19,000 to 70,600. During this same time period the percentage of the national income from agriculture dropped from 31.3 percent to 12.2 percent, while the percentage of the national income from manufacturing increased from 11.9 percent to 23.8 percent.

Improvement in the economy is further reflected by an improved standard of living. Life expectancy has increased from 46 to 70 years. Infant mortality has dropped from 113 to 41.7 deaths per thousand births. The percentage of occupied houses with electricity has risen from 28.8 percent to 80.6 percent. The number of telephones in use has grown from 16,000 to 170,000. Similarly, the number of registered automobiles has risen from 25,000 to more than a quarter of a million. It is estimated that today there is almost one automobile or truck for every ten Puerto Ricans.[39]

To a large extent, the improvement in the standard of living of the Puerto Rican people can be attributed to the role assumed by the government since the Popular Democratic party has been in control. The Populares have employed two basic means to better the living conditions of the populace. The first has been to attract outside industries to the island. Through the Puerto Rico Industrial

[39] All of the above data are taken from Junta de Plantificación, *Indicadores económicos de Puerto Rico*, February, 1965.

Development Corporation, popularly known as Fomento, the government has provided lucrative inducements to outside investors. These include exemption from insular taxes for as long as twenty-five years, the building of the factories, recruitment and training of local personnel, and technical assistance. By 1964, Fomento had directly promoted or assisted 900 factories. The percentage of the net income originating in manufacturing that came from Fomento plants rose from 3.5 percent in 1950 to 62.6 percent in 1964. Of the 91,000 Puerto Ricans employed in manufacturing in 1964, 60,000 (or about two-thirds) were employees of Fomento-inspired plants.[40]

To better conditions, a large portion of government expenditure has been devoted to the areas of education, health, and public welfare. In relation to its gross national product, Puerto Rico spent more in 1964 for education and health services than any other country in the world.[41] The commonwealth government and the local municipalities have also put much money into public housing and public works in order to provide cheap housing, better roads, and public facilities. In 1964, 22 percent of the housing units built were government owned.[42]

Since World War II Puerto Rico has experienced an almost uninterrupted growth in its economy. Agriculture has become subordinate to industry in its relative importance to the economy. A welfare-oriented government has increased the number of schools, teachers, pupils, health facilities, and public housing units. The result has been a steady increase in the standard of living for most of the populace.

The other aspect of the Puerto Rican economy is American domination. Americans on the mainland developed an economic interest in the island shortly after Puerto Rico fell into American hands. As of 1930, 60 percent of the banking concerns and the public utilities were controlled by Americans. Eighty percent of the tobacco industry and 100 percent of the steamship lines were

---

[40] Junta de Plantificación, *Informe económico al gobernador*, 1964, pp. 21, 28.
[41] *Ibid.*, p. 122.
[42] *Ibid.*, p. 47.

Yankee dominated.[43] By the 1960's the situation had not changed to a great extent. According to government sources as reported by Gordon Lewis, ". . . 70 percent of all investment in the economy is made by outside American interests and . . . only one out of every four factories is in Puerto Rican hands. Nor is that offset by a sizeable degree of Puertoricanization of the managerial operation of the plants. The percentage of Puerto Ricans in the top echelons of the managerial elite was somewhat less than 20 percent in 1958."[44] As of 1964, two out of three of the factories sponsored by Fomento were owned by non–Puerto Ricans.[45] Moreover, existing and profitable Puerto Rican–owned enterprises are being purchased by American investors. Once these firms leave Puerto Rican ownership, the profits, for the most part, are sent back to the United States. Such investments also fail to assume the traditional role of foreign investments—to build up underdeveloped areas of the economy.

The nature of the trade to and from the island also indicates American domination. Almost all the goods exported from Puerto Rico are sent to the United States; almost all imported goods come from the United States. In addition, all the goods shipped between the United States and Puerto Rico are transported on American-owned ships, according to the requirements of federal law.[46] The Puerto Rican economy is thus becoming, in essence, a subsidiary of the economy of the United States.

The consequences of the relationships between these two economies are manifold. In a relatively short period of time Puerto Rico has moved from a predominantly agrarian to a consumer-oriented economy without going through the traditional process of industrialization that characterized the economic development of the United States and western Europe. Puerto Rican industries tend to be distributive outlets and assembling points for American enterprises. A typical example is the Ford assembly plant. Ameri-

---

[43] Lewis, *Freedom and Power*, p. 87.

[44] *Ibid.*, p. 211.

[45] Anderson, *Party Politics*, p. 8.

[46] Junta de Plantificación, *Informe económico al gobernador*, 1964, pp. 72–81.

can supermarkets and department stores are located throughout the metropolitan areas of the island. The Puerto Rican middle class that has emerged to service this economy consists of clerks, salesmen, managers, and public relations personnel instead of technicians and independent businessmen. The interests as well as the future of this class tie them to the mainland economy and society rather than to their native Puerto Rico.[47] (In several respects, this situation is parallel to that of Czarist Russia on the eve of the revolution. That economy had "skipped" a stage, leading industries were in the hands of foreigners, and the native middle class was weak. The bourgeoisie were incapable of leading a nationalist revolution).[48]

Despite the growth and expansion of the economy, Puerto Rico is beset by two troublesome problems: unemployment and a large per capita debt. During the last thirteen years, unemployment has remained in the vicinity of 13 percent.[49] Other estimates have placed the unemployment rate at closer to 30 percent, taking into account those who are employable but no longer seek work.[50] In addition, unemployment is most heavily concentrated in the 14–24 age group.[51] Regardless of what measure of unemployment is most used, the problem takes on an added dimension when the figures of net migration from the island are considered. According to government sources, Puerto Rico, with a population of about 2.5 million, has since 1950 exported nearly 500,000 of its people to the United States. In recent years the annual number has dropped below 5,000.[52] If Puerto Rico was unable to resolve its unemployment problems when large emigration was taking place, it does not seem likely that she will be able to do so when the emigration has nearly ceased.

[47] Lewis, *Freedom and Power*, pp. 191–197. Cf. Curtis, *Land Reform, Democracy, and Economic Interest*, pp. 17–18.

[48] Leon Trotsky, *The History of the Russian Revolution*, pp. 10–12.

[49] Reynolds and Gregory, *Wages, Productivity, and Industrialization*, p. 38.

[50] Wagenheim, "Kinship or Colony," p. 8.

[51] Junta de Plantificación, *Informe económico al gobernador*, 1964, pp. 147–148.

[52] *Ibid.*, p. 156.

In addition to unemployment, the Puerto Rican economy is heavily burdened by personal debt. In part, this is a function of buying American goods at American prices despite the fact that the wage level is below that of the mainland. One economist pointed out that the cost of living in San Juan is 12 percent higher than that in New York City, although the wage level in the area is considerably lower. It should be noted also that in Puerto Rico, as of 1963, 40 percent of the families receiving 13 percent of the national income had a yearly income of $1,850 or less.[53] In the decade from 1954 to 1964, consumer debt grew by 29 percent.[54]

A journey through the crowded San Juan metropolitan area provides visible testimony to the consumption orientation of Puerto Rican society. The stores, branches of such mainland concerns as Acme, Woolworth's, and Lerner's, are filled with the latest American goods. Every store usually has a sign notifying prospective customers of the availability of easy credit terms. The roads are clogged with late-model American cars. Television antennae proliferate across the rooftops of even the most dilapidated slum. Advertisements, which are to be found in any public place, call upon the populace to purchase and enjoy more of the latest products of the American economy.

The Puerto Rican society has had to pay a social price for this acquisitive economy. In the last five years, thefts have increased by nearly 50 percent. Drug addiction has quintupled in the last four years. It has been estimated that there is one drug addict for every 250 Puerto Ricans. At present Puerto Rico has the highest suicide rate of any Catholic country. The homicide rate is also increasing, as is the rate of mental disturbance.[55]

Puerto Rico's economic growth, by any standards, is impressive. However, the island's economy is virtually an appendage to that of the United States. Furthermore, the society is haunted by high

[53] *Ibid.*, p. 44.

[54] *Ibid.*, p. 108.

[55] Marques, *"El puertorriqueña dócil,"* p. 43; Kal Wagenheim, "Education in Puerto Rico," *San Juan Review*, 2, no. 5 (June, 1965), 8.

consumer debt, large unemployment, and the increasing social problems inherent to a growing and acquisitive economy.

THE POLITICAL ENVIRONMENT[56]

Two contradictory features characterize the political landscape of Puerto Rico. On the one hand, as one party has been in office since 1940, there has been stability on the island. On the other, the unresolved issue of the political status of Puerto Rico, the central concern of island politics, is a potential source of great instability.

Puerto Rico has been officially designated as a commonwealth of the United States since 1952. Puerto Ricans vote for their own governor and for members of both houses of their island's legislature. They are also citizens of the United States but cannot vote in national elections and have no representation in Congress. They do not pay income taxes but are eligible for draft into the armed forces of the United States. Few Puerto Ricans regard the commonwealth status as the final solution to the issue of political status. Proponents of the alternatives to commonwealth—independence or statehood—have been unable to persuade a majority of the voters to support their respective positions. All Puerto Ricans are well aware, however, that the United States will make the final decision. As under Spanish rule, the determination of the political status of the island rests in the hands of the metropolitan power and not in the hands of the Puerto Rican people.

Despite the undetermined status of the island, the years since 1940 have been marked by political stability. The Partido Popular Democrático (Popular Democratic party or PPD) came to power in that year and has remained in power up to the present. Since 1944 it has received approximately 60 percent of the vote in every island election. Its strength is relatively evenly distributed throughout the island. Thus, in addition to the governorship, the party controls large majorities in the insular legislature and in the munici-

---

[56] This section is heavily indebted to the penetrating work of Robert Anderson, *Party Politics in Puerto Rico*.

palities. In the last fourteen years, the PPD has controlled two-thirds of the Senate seats and three-quarters of the House seats. In order to assure minority representation at the national and municipal levels, legislation was passed (initiated by the PPD) guaranteeing the minority parties token representation. In essence, then, Puerto Rico is a one-and-a-half-party state with the one party, the PPD, firmly entrenched.[57]

At this point, it might be instructive to examine the political position and composition of the political parties that exist in Puerto Rico today. One characteristic common to the three major parties is an absence of ideology. According to Professor Anderson, "In Puerto Rico political parties have typically been nonideological, vague of program, and willing to work within the existing system."[58] They have been willing to compromise and unwilling, for the most part, to exclude any segment of the population from their ranks.

The PPD came into power as a semirevolutionary movement preaching extensive economic reform and social welfare. Although Muñoz Marín assured the voters that a vote for his party was not a vote for change in political status, it was well known that the PPD was predominantly oriented in the direction of independence. This proindependence sentiment, however, was not included in the party's platform. Since it has been in power, the PPD has gone through a transition. It is no longer a semirevolutionary movement, but a responsible governing party. Party sentiment on the status issue has shifted from the desire for independence to an acceptance of commonwealth status or some alternative form of permanent association with the United States. It has also taken a more conservative economic position. In 1940 the party pledged itself to eradicate exploitation. High taxes for the rich were advocated and extensive

[57] In the 1968 election, the PPD lost to the Progressive party, a newly organized statehood party headed by Luis Ferre. The PPD lost because Governor Sánchez bolted from the PPD and ran under the banner of a new party, the People's party. The 10 percent garnered by this party cost the PPD the election.

[58] Anderson, *Party Politics*, p. 48.

The Politics of Puerto Rican University Students

welfare measures were promised. Its shift toward pragmatism appears in the changed function of Fomento, the Puerto Rico Industrial Development Corporation. At first, Fomento began to operate its own factories, but it now has moved to a position where, in actuality, it subsidizes private investment. As the PPD has become more moderate, its base of support has widened. Originally, the main appeal of the PPD was addressed to the peasantry, and the party still draws a disproportionate amount of its vote from the rural areas. However, as the PPD's platform became more moderate and pragmatic, it began to attract the increasing support of the middle class, as well as maintaining a hold on the urban workers.

At this juncture of Puerto Rican history, the PPD is generally considered a liberal-centrist party. It is committed to the status quo and no longer offers radical solutions to the problems of Puerto Rico. However, since it is the largest party on the island, it contains within itself a variety of factions. These factions generally reflect the three alternatives for the resolution of the status issue: independence, association, and statehood.

TABLE 1

Percentage of Puerto Rican Votes by Party, 1940–1964

	PIP %	PPD %	PER %	PAC %	Socialist %
1940	—	38.0	24.0	—	15.0
1944	—	65.0	17.0	—	12.0
1948	11.0	61.0	14.0	—	10.0
1952	19.0	65.0	13.0	—	3.0
1956	12.0	63.0	25.0	—	—
1960	3.0	58.0	32.0	7.0	—
1964	3.0	59.0	35.0	3.0	

PIP—Independence
PPD—Popular Democrat
PER—Republican Statehood
PAC—Christian Action

As can be seen in Table 1, the PER or Partido Estadista Republicano (Republican Statehood party) is presently the major competitor of the PPD. Its fortunes have been steadily rising since 1952; in the 1964 election the PER garnered 35 percent of the vote. As its name indicates, this party is committed to the achievement of statehood for Puerto Rico. It is the only party on the island that is officially affiliated with a mainland party, in this case the Republican party. The PER is regarded as being on the right of the political spectrum because of its statehood position and its conservative economic program. The PER is a strong supporter of private enterprise and on occasion has advocated the curtailment of welfare programs. It derives its support from the wealthier elements of the business community and the newly prosperous segments of the middle class. In addition, it receives surprisingly strong support from the Negro community. In fact, the great historic leader of the PER was a Negro, José Celso Barbosa. (This support has been attributed to the fair treatment Negroes received during the early days of American rule.) Despite its conservative orientation, the PER has gained strength and may soon be in a position to challenge the PPD effectively.

The PIP or Partido Independentista Puertorriqueño (Puerto Rican Independence party) is the only party appearing on the ballot that advocates independence as a solution to the status question. As shown in Table 1, the party has of late fallen upon hard times. In the last election the PIP received 3 percent of the vote compared with the 19 percent it obtained in 1952, when it was the second largest party on the island. The PIP is considered to the left of the political spectrum. This placement is due almost solely to its position on independence, since in its other programs it is very similar to the PPD.

Politically, the PIP is in difficulty. It participates in a system whose very legitimacy it questions. However, unlike a radical splinter party, the PIP remains respectful, legalistic, and responsible. It functions as the *official* left and lends its presence to multi-party delegations and governmental commissions. In its official statements as well as in campaign oratory, the United States is rarely criticized, much less attacked. The PIP assures its supporters and potential voters of its unqualified admiration and affection for the United States. From the point of view of the PIP, independence has been defined as a way in which a meaningful Puerto Rican–American relationship can be maintained, if not strengthened. The PIP desires independence primarily to maintain the cultural identity of the Puerto Rican people. Its main base of support has come from intellectuals, some professionals, and ardent Catholics resentful of domination by a materialistic Protestant power. The PIP's recent setbacks have made its chances for revival, even for survival, appear quite slim.

The Movimento Pro-Independencia or MPI (Proindependence Movement), like the PIP, is committed to independence. But it does not recognize the legitimacy of the present political system. Without very much success, the MPI urged the Puerto Rican voters to boycott the last insular election. The MPI is the radical left of Puerto Rican politics. It does not politely request independence; it vehemently demands it as an inherent right. In order to further its cause, it engages in picketing and other forms of direct action, including the disruption of the island's Fourth of July festivities. The MPI has openly admired Fidel Castro, but in recognition of public feelings, it has recently asked its public speakers to underplay their ardor for him. The MPI opposes the role of the United States and American businessmen in the economy of Puerto Rico. It claims that Puerto Ricans are being exploited and that all industries on the island should therefore be nationalized in order to ensure justice and equality for all Puerto Ricans, especially the lower strata. The MPI not only opposes the policies of the United States in Puerto Rico, but it opposes the policies and practices of the United States in Latin America, Vietnam, and everywhere else in the world as well.

The MPI has received very little support, but it nonetheless considers itself to be the true political expression of the Puerto Rican people. Its failure to attract wider overt support, its leaders claim, is the result of brainwashing, fear of recriminations, and the vested interest of the bureaucracy and the wealthier classes. The MPI's failure to attract more support may also be attributed to its own failure to develop programs and analyses. The MPI leadership appears to be devoid of knowledge or interest about such matters as the working of the economy or the nature of the educational system. In recent years it has drifted from issue to issue, exerting little effort toward the drafting of a creative program. As a result, it has done little to calm the fears of large numbers of Puerto Ricans who think that an MPI victory would bring economic and social chaos in its wake. Until it can begin to discuss intelligently the nature of Puerto Rican society in the postindependent era, it can never hope to become a major force in the island's politics.

In 1960 the Partido Acción Cristiana or PAC (Christian Action party) appeared on the ballot for the first time. At that time it obtained 7 percent of the vote, but by 1964 it had dropped to 3 percent. The party is promoted by the Catholic hierarchy and its raison d'etre appears to be the maintenance and expansion of the Church and Catholicism on the island. The failure to attract more than 7 percent is a testimony to the Church's weak political hold on the populace. Even when the Church made opposition to the PPD a matter of religious obligation to Catholics in the 1960 election, the PPD still received 63 percent of the vote. The little support that it has received has been mainly at the expense of the Catholic supporters of the PIP. Most observers do not think that the PAC will survive much longer.

In reality there are only two political parties in Puerto Rico, the PPD, and the PER, each reflecting the principal alternatives to the problem of political status. Independence as a solution and parties supporting the drive for independence have lost the public support that they once had, largely because of the constant and pervasive equation made by the mass media and the leaders of the PPD and PER: "Independence equals economic and political chaos." The populace has become convinced that independence will endanger recent economic gains as well as the political tranquility of the island. Idealism and the concern for local culture and tradition have been subordinated to economics. As Richard Morse has said, "It seems strange that a people so proud of its Hispanic soul translates it into a dollar and cents accounting, carrying it down to the last decimal point."[59]

The Puerto Rican university students of today are the products of their historic, cultural, economic, and political environments. There is, however, little within these environments that would predispose them toward idealism and nationalism. Puerto Ricans have always looked abroad for their economic survival and the political decisions that affected their lives. Their contact with the world has effectively been limited to Spain and the United States. The society of which the students are a part is predominantly materialistic, but it has been only in the last generation that material benefits have been accessible to large segments of the populace. The concern for economic betterment appears to have deafened the ears of the people to the isolated cries of intellectuals and radical politicians who call for independence and the maintenance of a Puerto Rican culture.

POLITICAL POSTURE OF THE UNIVERSITY STUDENTS IN PUERTO RICO[60]

What is the political nature of the students at the University of Puerto Rico who have emerged from such an environment and such a history? Table 2 reveals the political party choices of Puerto Rican students in 1956 and in 1964. In both of these years, a near majority of the students preferred the governing PPD, the center party. More interesting, though, is the fact that, of the remainder, more chose the conservative PER than the somewhat leftist PIP. In both years, the supporters of the PIP were a minority on the Río Piedras campus, representing less than one-quarter of the student body.

An interesting fact emerges when the distribution of the students' political responses is compared with that of the island's total electorate in 1956 and 1964. Whereas the national electorate's

59 Morse, "La transformación ilusoria," p. 369.

60 The data presented in this section and all other data pertaining to students at the University of Puerto Rico are derived from the Comparative National Development Project of the Institute of International Studies, University of California, Berkeley, California. See Appendix I *re* methodology.

TABLE 2
Party Preference of Puerto Rican University Students in 1956† and 1964

	1956 %	1964 %
PIP	23	24
PPD	47	47
PER	30	26
PAC	—	2
N	505	558

† The 1956 data are obtained from Peter Bachrach, "Attitudes toward Authority and Party Preference in Puerto Rico," *Public Opinion Quarterly*, 22 (1958), 71–72.

support for the PIP declined from 12 percent to 3 percent during those years, the proportion of students favoring the PIP remained relatively constant at about one-quarter. This means that in the latter year the proportion supporting the PIP at the university was eight times as great as it was among the voting public. Thus, compared with the voters, the students in Puerto Rico can be regarded as more to the left. It is important, however, to keep in mind the reference group used. Although the left as represented by the student supporters of the PIP appears large compared with the island's electorate, it is a minority position on campus and ranks third behind the PPD and the PER.

Another measure of the political position of the students is the student's own assessment of his political position compared with that of his fellow students. On this variable as well close to a majority (46%) felt that they were somewhere in the middle. Again the right has more support than the left. Thirty-two percent classify themselves to the right of most of their peers, whereas only 21 percent consider themselves to the left of their fellow students.

In Latin America, probably the best comparative indicator of an individual's political position is his opinion of Fidel Castro and the Cuban Revolution, which have rallied and divided students throughout the continent. He and his revolution have come to symbolize the left: revolutionary overthrow of an oligarchy, independence from the sphere of the United States, mobilization of a populace to eradicate hunger and illiteracy, and modernization of a society. In

Puerto Rico only 10 percent of the students reported favorable feelings toward the Cuban Revolution, and only 5 percent agreed with Castro's ideas and actions. It is interesting to note that Mexican students, coming from a somewhat different environment and political tradition, differed in their assessment of Castro and the Cuban Revolution.[61] Forty-six percent of these students were favorable toward the Cuban Revolution and 37 percent agreed with the ideas and actions of Fidel Castro.

Comparison of Puerto Rican and Mexican students on attitudes toward the United States and Russia affords similar findings. Eighty percent of the Puerto Rican students reported that the United States was the country toward which they felt most favorable, whereas 2 percent said the USSR and 1 percent said Red China. Among the Mexican students, 39 percent replied the United States, whereas 11 percent said the Soviet Union and 2 percent answered Red China.

In terms of student political activities, the number of students varied by the type of activity. Forty-five percent of those who answered said that they had voted in the last elections in their school, and 29 percent had attended a meeting of the student council. When the activity escalated to a different level, the numbers of participating students dropped. Seventy-eight percent had never participated in a strike or demonstration, but 13 percent had participated in at least one. Only 5 percent identified themselves as members of a student political party.

On March 26, 1965, students at the University of Puerto Rico were asked to vote in a referendum concerning the regulation of student activities on the campus. This was the first time in about seventeen years that the student body had had the opportunity to speak directly to the faculty and administration about a political matter. The two alternatives on which they were asked to vote were: (a) "The freedom of expression, association, and assembly that are in the Constitution are guaranteed to students on the campus";

[61] All data pertaining to Mexican students are derived from Comparative National Development Project of the Institute of International Studies, University of California, Berkeley, California, and Harvard University.

and (b) "The freedom of expression, association, and assembly that are in the Constitution are guaranteed to students on the campus, but political activities should be regulated. Demonstrations, pickets, and public meetings on the campus that disturb scholarly activities or are contrary to the norms of the institution are prohibited." Alternative (b) won by better than a two-to-one margin, 2,963 to 1,375. This means that more than two out of three students voting were in favor of placing restrictions on their own political activities.

In Puerto Rican student politics the left is far from being a dominant force on the Río Piedras campus. Almost a majority take the safe middle position, and the right seems to have more support than the left.[62] The negative attitude toward Castro and the Cuban Revolution coupled with a positive attitude toward the United States is further evidence of the nonradical nature of the Puerto Rican students. On the basis of these data, the Puerto Rican student body as a whole may be considered to be in a center-conservative political position.

As indicated initially, the central concern of this study is to determine the factors that have a major impact upon the political attitudes and behavior of students at the University of Puerto Rico. The study of the political behavior of university students cannot be conducted *in vacuo*. A center-conservative student body like the Puerto Ricans can be better understood when the historical and political context within which they were socialized is known. A colonial society that has never in its history rebelled, in which indigenous institutions capable of supporting a strong nationalist movement have been weak or attenuated, and in which the economy, the polity, and the value system are thoroughly dominated by an outside power does not, it would appear, breed a radical student body.

[62] Many of the faculty, administration, and student body interviewed felt that a right-wing student group on any given occasion could attract more support than any left-wing group. In the case of the referendum, left-wing activist students campaigned for it and right-wing activist students against it.

Chapter II

RECRUITMENT TO HIGHER EDUCATION
IN PUERTO RICO

In order to gain a better understanding of the political attitudes of
university students in Puerto Rico, it is necessary to know who they
are and the factors related to their entering institutions of higher
learning. There is no need at this point to relate specific findings to
the students' politics, but a close look at the Puerto Rican educational system, both in itself and in comparison with the United
States and other Latin American countries, should bring out circumstances involved in getting from elementary school to university that will be relevant to later analysis.

Puerto Ricans maintain a deep commitment to education. Puerto
Rico leads Latin America in the percentage of its school-age population actually enrolled.[1] Table 3 reveals that of those aged 15–19, 77
percent attend school in Puerto Rico, compared with 53 percent in
Costa Rica, 51 percent in Venezuela, 50 percent in Panama, 49 percent in Chile, and 39 percent in Mexico. In the continental United
States during 1960–1961, 89 percent of the 5–20 age cohort attended
school.[2] Puerto Rico is thus almost equal to the United States in
terms of the percentage of the school-age population attending
school.

This enrollment ratio becomes even more impressive when the
per capita income figures of Puerto Rico are compared with those

[1] Center of Latin American Studies, *Statistical Abstract of Latin America,
1963*, p. 28.
[2] U.S. Bureau of the Census, *Statistical Abstract of the United States, 1964*,
p. 110.

TABLE 3

*Percentage of Persons Aged 5–19 Attending School and Per Capita Income
for Puerto Rico and Latin American Countries about 1960*

Country	Percent of 5–19 Enrolled	Per Capita Income $(U.S.)
Puerto Rico	77	685
Costa Rica	53	291
Venezuela	51	566
Panama	51	367
Chile (1957)	49	507
Argentina	48	360
Paraguay	48	116
Dominican Republic	45	228
Mexico	39	279
Peru	39	145
Ecuador	38	130
Cuba (1956/7)	38	340
Brazil	36	129
Colombia	34	213
El Salvador	32	176
Nicaragua	26	—
Honduras	24	182
Guatemala	22	151
Haiti	17	72
Bolivia (1956)	17	66

Source: Center of Latin American Studies, *Statistical Abstract of Latin
America, 1963*, pp. 28, 80.

of the United States and the Latin American countries. (See Table
3.) Puerto Rico, with a per capita income of $685, sends almost as
many of its school-age population to school as the United States,
with a per capita income of $2,307. This is true despite the fact that
Puerto Rico has a lower legal compulsory school age (14) than any
state in the United States.[3] Puerto Rico, whose per capita income is
21 percent higher than that of Venezuela, sends 50 percent more of
its population aged 5–19 to school than Venezuela. Also, Puerto
Rico devotes a higher percentage of its national income to public
school expenditure than other Latin American countries, the Unit-

[3] Luis Nieves Falcón, *Recruitment to Higher Education in Puerto Rico,
1940–1960*, p. 27; Junta de Plantificación, *Informe económico al gobernador*,
1964, p. 120.

TABLE 4

*Percentage of Puerto Ricans Agreeing That Education
is the Only Avenue for Social Mobility*

Responses to: "Persons of my social
class can improve their positions in
life only by increasing the amount of
schooling they get."

	Years of School				
	0	1–4	5–8	9–12	13+
Agree	94	93	88	72	64
Undecided	3	2	1	3	1
Disagree	3	5	11	25	35
Total	100	100	100	100	100
	=238	=287	=224	=165	=75

Total Sample — 989

Source: *Social Class and Social Change in Puerto Rico*, by Melvin Tumin with Arnold Feldman (Copyright © 1961 by Princeton University Press): Table on p. 108. Reprinted with the permission of the publisher.

ed States, countries of western Europe, Japan, Israel, or New Zealand.[4]

At the level of university education only the United States and the USSR in 1960 surpassed Puerto Rico in the number of college students per thousand of the population.[5] If the age cohort 20–24 is used as a base, Puerto Rico ranks fourth behind the United States, the Philippines, and Australia in the percentage attending colleges or universities.[6]

Melvin Tumin's study, *Social Class and Social Change in Puerto Rico*, reveals that a high positive evaluation of education permeates all social classes in Puerto Rico.[7] In response to the statement "Every father has the obligation to send his children to school for at least 8 years, no matter what sacrifices this may entail," 93 percent of the respondents agreed.[8] Table 4, taken from Tumin's study,

[4] UNESCO, *Basic Facts and Figures: International Statistics Relating to Education, Culture, and Mass Communications*, pp. 72–79.

[5] *Ibid.*, pp. 53–57, 170–175.

[6] Seymour M. Lipset, *First New Nation*, p. 260.

[7] Melvin Tumin with Arnold Feldman, *Social Class and Social Change in Puerto Rico*, pp. 107, 109.

[8] *Ibid.*, p. 107.

shows the importance placed on education as the *sole* means of improving one's lot in life. Eighty-seven percent of the entire sample agreed; at the lower end of the educational scale agreement was nearly unanimous.

These behavioral and attitudinal indicators not only illustrate the high regard that Puerto Ricans have for education and its benefits. The fact that both Puerto Rico and the Philippines rank so high among nations of the world in terms of the proportion of the age cohort attending college is further testimony of the influence of the United States upon the educational systems and the attitudes toward education in these two former possessions.

FILTERING PROCESS

Despite the commitment to education in Puerto Rico, many Puerto Ricans do not enter secondary school, and more are never admitted to college. As in every educational system in the Western Hemisphere, a filtering process takes place as students move through the educational system.

Only 25 percent of the Puerto Rican students who entered the first grade in 1952–1953 were in the twelfth grade eleven years later. The major difficulty in retaining students seems to be at the secondary level. Seventy-two percent of those who began the first grade in 1955–1956 completed six years of schooling. But of those beginning the seventh grade, only 42 percent reached the twelfth during the same time period.[9]

However, Puerto Rico again compares favorably with the rest of Latin America. In the most advanced Latin American countries, about 25 percent of those beginning primary school complete it, and of those going on to secondary school, about 32 percent finish. In these same countries only 5 percent of those who start elementary school finish secondary.[10] The data for the individual countries

[9] Department of Public Education, Puerto Rico, "Poder de retención de las escuelas de Puerto Rico," September, 1961 (mimeo), pp. 8, 11; Consejo Superior de Enseñanza, *Podrá mi hijo ingresar en la universidad*, p. 26.

[10] Office of Education, U.S. Department of Health, Education, and Welfare, *The Current Situation in Latin American Education*, pp. 21–22.

of Latin America starkly illustrate the weakness of their educational systems. In Brazil, as of 1960, about half of those aged 7–11 had never been inside a schoolhouse, and fewer than 10 percent of those enrolled got beyond four years of school.[11] In Mexico, as of 1956, for every 1,000 who began primary education there were about 460 who never had access to any education. Of the 1,000 who did begin, 471 did not reach the second grade, and only 59 commenced secondary school. Of these only 6 went on to higher education.[12]

Table 5 details the percentage of students in various Latin American countries who complete primary and secondary educations. None of the countries approaches the Puerto Rican figure of 72 percent completing primary education. Only Costa Rica, at the secondary level, surpasses the Puerto Rican retention rate of 42 percent. This can be attributed to the facts that the selectivity of the Costa Rican secondary school system takes only 22 percent of the primary school population, and that Costa Rica's secondary school lasts five years, compared with six for Puerto Rico.[13]

However, comparison with the educational system of the United States reveals the inadequacy of the Puerto Rican educational system in terms of its ability to keep a student in school from the first to the twelfth grades. Twenty-five percent of Puerto Rican children who start the first grade finish the twelfth, compared with 70 percent of American students.[14] Nor does Puerto Rico fare as well as the United States in the number of high school graduates who go on to college. In 1959–1960, 22 percent of Puerto Rican high school graduates entered institutions of higher learning. In the United

[11] Frank Bonilla, "Brazil," in *Education and Political Development*, ed. James S. Coleman, p. 198.

[12] Kalman H. Silvert, "The University Student," in *Continuity and Change in Latin America*, ed. John J. Johnson, p. 208.

[13] Oscar Vera, "The Educational Situation and Requirements in Latin America," in *Social Aspects of Economic Developments in Latin America*, vol. 1, ed. Egbert DeVries and José Medina Echavarría, p. 291.

[14] Office of Education, U.S. Department of Health, Education, and Welfare, *Digest of Educational Statistics, 1965*, p. 124.

TABLE 5

*Percentage of Pupils Completing Primary and Secondary Courses
in Certain Latin American Countries*

Country	Length of Course in Years	Period	Percentage Completing Course
Primary Education			
†Puerto Rico	6	1955–1960	72
Chile	6	1951–1956	25
Venezuela	6	1953/54–58/59	23
Costa Rica	6	1950–1955	22
Brazil	4	1956–1959	19
Peru	6	1950–1955	18
Colombia	5	1954–1958	14
Secondary Education			
Costa Rica	5	1952–1956	56
†Puerto Rico	6	1955–1960	42
Venezuela	5	1954/55–58/59	30
Peru	5	1951–1955	28
Chile	6	1951–1956	27

Source: Vera, "Educational Situation and Requirements," p. 291.
†Puerto Rican data come from the Department of Public Education, Puerto
Rico, "Poder de retención de las escuelas de Puerto Rico," pp. 8, 11.

States during the same period, about 53 percent of the high school
graduates entered institutions of higher learning.[15]

One of the factors accounting for the small percentage of high
school graduates going on to universities, compared with the United
States, is that the high school graduate population has increased
faster than the number of available university places. Much political pressure is being applied to both the chancellor of the University of Puerto Rico and the secretary of education to establish
junior colleges at various regional centers around the island.[16] The
University of Puerto Rico, the island's largest and most prestigious
institution, accounts for twenty-nine out of every forty places for
college freshmen in Puerto Rico.[17] In the fall of 1964, about 67 per-

[15] Falcón, *Recruitment to Higher Education*, p. 77; Office of Education, *Educational Statistics, 1965*, p. 124.

[16] *San Juan Star*, July 7, 1965.

[17] Falcón, *Recruitment to Higher Education*, p. 77; Consejo Superior de Enseñanza, *Podrá mi hijo ingresar en la universidad*, pp. 1, 35.

cent of all college students working toward a degree attended the University of Puerto Rico.[18] However, the University of Puerto Rico was forced to deny admittance to more than half the qualified applicants during the period from 1955 to 1964.

Once the student enters a university or college, the problem is to remain until graduation. At the University of Puerto Rico during the years 1955–1960, 45 to 50 percent of the freshmen did not graduate.[19] Throughout Latin America the dropout rate is generally higher. In Mexico five out of six who enter the university fail to graduate. At the University of Buenos Aires, the largest university in all Latin America, the dropout rate is very high. It varies by school, however, with architecture having a rate of 80 percent, law of 64 percent, and medicine of 44 percent.[20] In the United States, an estimated 40 percent of those who go on to college eventually obtain a degree.[21]

In the comparison of school systems thus far, the Puerto Rican system seems to be closer to that of the United States than to those of other Latin American countries. In the availability of education and in the use of education by the population, Puerto Rico more resembles the open, nearly universal system of the United States than the semiclosed, elitist pattern of most of Latin America.

DETERMINANTS OF ENTRANCE TO HIGHER EDUCATION

That sector of the school-age population which does make it through the school system is not randomly distributed, even in a relatively open system like that of Puerto Rico. There are several

[18] Office of Education, U.S. Department of Health, Education, and Welfare, *Opening (Fall) Enrollment in Higher Education, 1964*, pp. 80–81. There are now four other institutions of higher learning in Puerto Rico: the Catholic University of Puerto Rico, College of the Sacred Heart (all girls), Inter-American University of Puerto Rico, and Puerto Rico Junior College. In the fall of 1964, there were enrolled and working toward a degree 3,876; 302; 5,971; and 1,289 respectively. The University of Puerto Rico at the same time had an enrollment of 23,972.

[19] Falcón, *Recruitment to Higher Education*, p. 142.

[20] Silvert, "University Student," p. 214.

[21] Harold R. W. Benjamin, *Higher Education in the American Republics*, p. 173.

important factors associated with a student's chances of admittance to an institution of higher education.

Urban versus Rural

One of the most important educational filters is the area of the parents' residence. Throughout Latin America an urban or rural residence is virtually the only variable necessary to predict whether or not a student will attend a university. In Latin America there is in general a strong correlation between percent rural and percent literate and percent of age cohort attending school.[22]

Data for selected countries grimly contrast the educational experiences of urban and rural populations. In Colombia during the period 1954–1958, 32 percent of the urban children attending primary school completed the program, as opposed to 0.5 percent of the rural children.[23] Myron Glazer reveals similar findings for urban and rural provinces in Chile. He also asserts that there is not one son of a peasant in attendance at the University of Chile.[24] In Venezuela, as of 1958, the state of rural education was so poor as to be virtually nonexistent.[25] At the University of Buenos Aires about 83 percent of the students came from Buenos Aires and its environs; only 2 percent were born in towns with less than 2,000 population.[26] According to a sample selected from two leading Mexican universities, only 7 percent of the student body spent their adolescence in rural areas or small towns.[27] Apparently the chances of the rural born or raised reaching the university are very slim indeed, and the overwhelming proportion of students in colleges or universities are urban born or bred.

[22] Center of Latin American Studies, *Statistical Abstract of Latin America, 1963*, p. 28. Costa Rica is the major exception to this generalization (Vera, "Educational Situation and Requirements," pp. 283, 284, 289).

[23] Vera, "Educational Situation and Requirements," p. 291.

[24] Myron Glazer, "The Professional and Political Attitudes of Chilean University Students," Ph.D. dissertation, Princeton University, 1965, p. 89.

[25] Office of Education, U.S. Department of Health, Education, and Welfare, *The Development of Education in Venezuela*, pp. 103–104.

[26] Silvert, "University Student," pp. 213–214.

[27] Comparative National Development Project, "Mexico," 1965 (mimeo), p. 3.

The Puerto Rican pattern is similar to that of the Latin American countries. During the latter 1950's, 96 out of every 100 in the urban zones completed elementary school, compared with 58 out of every 100 for the rural areas.[28] Table 6, derived from the 1960

TABLE 6

Percentage of Urban and Rural Males, Ages 5–34,
Enrolled in School in Puerto Rico in 1960

Males, 5 to 34 Years	% Urban (Total Enrolled 136,800)	% Rural (Total Enrolled 170,752)
5 years	18	9
6 years	53	38
7 years	78	68
8 years	84	80
9 years	88	83
10 years	93	89
11 years	93	87
12 years	90	83
13 years	86	76
14 years	80	65
15 years	74	54
16 years	66	44
17 years	55	33
18 years	44	24
19 years	34	17
20 years	26	10
21 years	22	7
22 years	17	7
23 years	14	6
24 years	15	8
25 to 29 years	11	6
30 to 34 years	7	4

Source: U.S. Bureau of Census, *Census of Population: 1960*, vol. 1, *Characteristics of the Population*, part 53, "Puerto Rico."

United States Census, indicates the percentage difference in attendance at school for various age groups of urban and rural males. At each age level a larger percentage of urban than rural males are in attendance at school. Moreover, of those in school, once past the

[28] Falcón, *Recruitment to Higher Education*, p. 48.

first few grades urban males are more likely to be farther along in school than rural males of the same age.[29]

According to Tumin's study, this difference in educational attainment between urban and rural children cannot be attributed to the low value placed on education by rural families.[30] More important is the financial strain caused by keeping a child in school. This strain is differentially experienced because rural families have less income than urban families. In 1959 the median income of urban males fourteen years and older was $1,497, compared with $658 for their rural peers.[31]

The quantitative and qualitative differences between the urban and rural school systems in Puerto Rico also help to explain the relative lack of academic achievement by the rural residents. Tumin's data indicate that the distance from home to a school was the reason given by a sizable number of rural respondents as to why their children had not completed school.[32] Also, a great many rural schools do not provide students with the facilities to complete their elementary education; many rural students attend schools that do not go beyond the third or fourth grades.

The difference in quality of the teachers in the urban and rural areas should be taken into account as well. In 1958–1959, 7 percent of the school teachers in the urban areas had less than two years of college, compared with 32 percent of those who taught in the rural zones. Furthermore, compared with the urban schools, rural schools lacked trained counselors, janitorial services, equipment, proper lighting, and recreational areas.[33]

It is not surprising to find that among freshmen at the University of Puerto Rico, urban students outnumbered rural students, despite the fact that the majority of eighteen year olds in Puerto Rico have a rural residence. Specifically, 89 percent of the freshmen class was

29 U.S. Bureau of the Census, *U.S. Census of Population: 1960*, vol. 1, *Characteristics of the Population*, part 53, "Puerto Rico."

30 Tumin, *Social Class and Social Change*, pp. 90–91.

31 *U.S. Census of Population: 1960*, "Puerto Rico."

32 Tumin, *Social Class and Social Change*, pp. 118–119.

33 Falcón, *Recruitment to Higher Education*, pp. 45–47.

from urban areas in 1960–1961, whereas 56 percent of all Puerto Ricans eighteen years of age reported a rural residence. This percentage has remained fairly constant since 1944–1945.[34]

Sex

An interesting factor that distinguishes Puerto Rico from both the United States and other Latin American countries is the role of sex in the recruitment to higher education. Contrary to indications elsewhere, sex does not appear to play a major part in the decision to go on to a university in Puerto Rico.

In the fall of 1964, of the 35,410 students working toward a university degree in Puerto Rico, 17,874, or slightly more than 50 percent, were women. At the same time in the United States, of the nearly 5 million working toward a degree, 39 percent were women.[35] It should be noted, however, that in Puerto Rico the female–male ratio of those graduating from high school tends to be greater than the female–male ratio of those attending college. This suggests that sex continues to be a factor in determining who goes to college, but it is not nearly as important in Puerto Rico as in other societies.[36] Melvin Tumin's study reveals the value that Puerto Ricans place on girls' education. This is particularly so in the case of the educated Puerto Ricans. Tumin found that about 80 percent of his respondents who had gone beyond high school in their education disagreed with the statement that "formal education has much less practical value for girls than boys."[37]

The male–female split at the university level is much sharper in Latin America. In 1958, 75 percent of the students attending the University of Buenos Aires were men.[38] At the University of Chile

---

[34] *Ibid.*, p. 81.

[35] Office of Education, *Opening (Fall) Enrollment in Higher Education, 1964*, pp. 3, 80. The percentage of females attending the University of Puerto Rico has steadily increased since World War II (Falcón, *Recruitment to Higher Education*, p. 79).

[36] Leila Sussman, "High School to University in Puerto Rico," Social Science Research Center, University of Puerto Rico, 1965 (mimeo), pp. 75, 77, 78.

[37] Tumin, *Social Class and Social Change*, p. 111.

[38] Silvert, "University Student," p. 213.

in Santiago, Glazer's random selection in four of the faculties found 75 percent of his respondents to be male.[39] In the Comparative National Development Project, 78 percent of the students sampled at major universities in Mexico and Colombia were men.[40] In Costa Rica 35 percent of the students were female. In El Salvador the percentage of females was 17 percent, and in Nicaragua only 11 percent of the 2,052 students were female.[41]

The fact that about half the university students in Puerto Rico and at the Río Piedras campus of the University of Puerto Rico are women means that the educational milieu in Puerto Rico is different from that of both Latin America and the United States. The implication of this sex ratio for the political attitudes of university students will be considered later.

Socioeconomic Class

In general, the single best predictor of whether or not a student will attend college is the socioeconomic class of his father. The higher the class, the greater is the likelihood of attendance at a college or a university.

Table 7 indicates the percentage distribution of university students in Puerto Rico, the United States, and selected Latin American countries by the occupation of the students' fathers.[42] There is a larger percentage of students from blue-collar families at the Uni-

[39] Glazer, "Chilean University Students," p. 62.

[40] Comparative National Development Project, "Colombia," 1965 (mimeo), p. 1; *idem*, "Mexico," 1965 (mimeo), p. 1.

[41] Benjamin, *Higher Education*, p. 124.

[42] The data concerning the socioeconomic origins of the university students in Puerto Rico are derived from the University of Puerto Rico enrollments. As previously mentioned, more than two-thirds of the university population in Puerto Rico attends the University of Puerto Rico. Unfortunately, there are no data available on the socioeconomic background of students attending other colleges and universities on the island. Data from Leila Sussman's study indicate that the socioeconomic distribution of freshmen attending the UPR and those attending institutions of higher education elsewhere are not very dissimilar. The sample for her study, however, was a random stratified sample of high school seniors in Puerto Rico. Information as to whether or not they attended college was obtained from their high school principals in the autumn of 1965 (Sussman, "High School to University," pp. 94–95).

TABLE 7

Social Origin of University Students in Selected Countries

Countries	Occupation of Student's Father	
	Manual %	Nonmanual %
Puerto Rico: U.P.R. 1952[a]	25	75
U.P.R. 1960[b]	27	73
United States: 1958[b]	30	70
Mexico: Nacional Autónoma 1949[a]	12	88
Nacional Autónoma 1964[c]		
Universidad de Guanajuato 1964[c]	7	93
Argentina: U. of Buenos Aires 1958[b]	12	88
Brazil: U. of São Paulo 1959[b]	10	90
Colombia: Nacional U. 1960[d]	10	90
1964[e]	3	97
Peru: Lima[b]	16	84
San Marcos 1957[b]		
Chile: U. of Chile 1964[f]	10	90

Sources:

[a] Falcón, *Recruitment to Higher Education,* p. 91.
[b] R. Havighurst, "Latin American and North American Higher Education," *Comparative Education Review,* 4, no. 3 (February, 1961), 177.
[c] Comparative National Development Project, "Mexico," June, 1965.
[d] Robert C. Williamson, *El estudiante colombiano y sus actitudes,* p. 70.
[e] Comparative National Development Project, "Colombia," June, 1965.
[f] Glazer, "Chilean University Students," p. 57.

versity of Puerto Rico than at any university in the six Latin American countries listed. The percentage of working-class students attending institutions of higher learning in the United States is slightly higher. Puerto Rico more closely resembles the United States than Latin American countries in its proportion of blue-collar students in universities. This is further testimony to the fact of the openness of the Puerto Rican educational system.

A more intensive look at the occupational structure of Puerto Rico compared with the distribution of occupations among the fathers of the 1960–1961 freshmen class at the University of Puerto Rico (Table 8) reveals that, despite its relative openness, class does affect the chances of receiving a university education. The data show that although only 28 percent of the freshmen come from working-class and farm-worker families, these groups in 1960 in

TABLE 8

*Occupational Breakdown of Puerto Rican Labor Force
and Fathers of College Freshmen†*

Occupational Groups	Occupational Composition of Puerto Rico in 1960	Occupational Composition of Fathers of College Freshmen
	%	%
Professionals, semiprofessionals, proprietors, and managers of large businesses	11	25
White-collar workers	11	24
Small business	4	16
Skilled worker	18	15
Semi and unskilled worker	27	12
Farm owner and manager	5	7
Farm laborer and farm foreman	23	1
Other	1	1
Total	100	101*
	(N = 332,336)	(N = 1,749)

Source: Falcón, *Recruitment to Higher Education*, p. 83.
† The breakdown includes employed males, twenty-five years old and over, in Puerto Rican labor force in 1960, and fathers of college freshmen in a bachelor's program in 1960–1961 at the University of Puerto Rico, Río Piedras campus.
* Total does not equal 100 due to rounding off of percentages. In all succeeding tables, such a variation will simply be indicated by an asterisk (*).

Puerto Rico constituted more than two-thirds of the labor force. This means that the Puerto Rican working class and farm laborers were contributing only about 42 percent of their relative proportion to the freshman class. When the blue-collar occupations are broken down into three occupational classifications, the data show that the farm laborers had the least representation in the university, with the semiskilled and unskilled worker next. The professionals, semiprofessionals, proprietors, managers, and white-collar occupations contributed twice their proportion to the freshman class. The group that contributed most disproportionately is the small businessmen, who sent almost four times their number to the university. In general, the chance of becoming a college student is highly dependent on the occupation of the father.

Tumin's study also illustrates the importance of class as a determinant of educational attainment.[43] The amount of family income is an important factor. Fifty-one percent of the reasons given by the parent respondent as to why their children had not finished school were economic in nature, specifically the lack of money. This response was true for parents in each educational group, although its frequency was inversely related to level of education of the parents.[44] Tumin discusses the relationship between income and free public education:

> For many Puerto Ricans the education of a child becomes a matter of considerable financial strain, even though there is free public education. Clothing, school supplies, possible earnings of child become factors. For a family at the barest level of subsistence, as many Puerto Rican families must be judged to be, education of children must be valued highly before the necessary sacrifices are likely to be undertaken. A type of providential thinking—planning for the future, and delaying gratifications now for oneself in preference for later gratifications for one's children—must precede any consideration of those sacrifices. But this type of thinking is hard to acquire unless one has some good reason to approach life in this way. And good reasons of this kind are themselves hard to come by unless one has somehow experienced the benefits of thinking in these terms.[45]

Nature of School

The nature of the schools that the student attends is another factor associated with entrance to the university. Whether the school is public or private is related to area of residence and socioeconomic class. There are few private schools in the rural areas. Most are located in the metropolitan areas, primarily the greater San Juan area. Furthermore, metropolitan schools charge tuition of between $350 and $450 per year.[46] Consequently, these schools are not available to families in the lower income brackets or to those not living in metropolitan areas.

[43] Tumin, *Social Class and Social Change*, pp. 116–140.
[44] *Ibid.*, pp. 117.
[45] *Ibid.*, p. 80.
[46] Jane Alderdice, "The Case for Private School," *San Juan Review*, 2, no. 5 (June, 1965), 48.

Why do families send their children to private schools that charge tuition, when there are free public schools available? The principal reason seems to be the belief that their children can obtain a better education in a private school, secular or religious, than in a public school.[47] Many families who want their children to enter either the University of Puerto Rico or universities in the States enroll their sons and daughters in private schools. Most of these private schools, including the Catholic schools, use English as the language of instruction. Many have higher standards than the average public school. As one father expressed it, ". . . the level of attainment that passes for satisfactory or even more than satisfactory in public schools here is not anywhere near stateside standards." One mother when asked replied: "First, the English. Second, the discipline. The education itself is very deficient."[48]

The success of the private schools can be measured in different ways. First, the percentage of students attending private schools has grown. In 1940–1941, about 4 percent of all students were in private schools. This percentage has now grown to about 9 to 10 percent in 1959–1960.[49] Second, the private schools have been more successful in retaining and graduating their students than the public schools.[50] Finally, success can be measured in terms of enrollment in the University of Puerto Rico, the most desirable institution of higher education on the island. Data based on random samples from the various colleges of the University of Puerto Rico show that 35 percent of the students in the sample attended private high schools. If this sample is representative, the private schools with enrollments of about 10 percent contribute proportionately three and one-half times their number to the University of Puerto Rico.[51]

[47] The only public schools with academic standards to rival the private schools were the grammar and high school operated by the University of Puerto Rico. Interviews with faculty members supported this conclusion.

[48] Alderdice, "Case for Private School," p. 48.

[49] Falcón, *Recruitment to Higher Education*, p. 27.

[50] Department of Public Education, "Poder de retención de las escuelas de Puerto Rico," pp. 8–15.

[51] This proportion of private school students attending the University of Puerto Rico is approximately two times larger than it was in 1944–1945 (Falcón, *Recruitment to Higher Education*, p. 80).

SUMMARY AND CONCLUSION

Education from primary school to the university is relatively more available for the school-age population of Puerto Rico than for that of any other Latin American country. A greater percentage of the age cohort attends school and remains longer than elsewhere in Latin America. Despite the fact that Puerto Rico can be considered a developing country, Puerto Rico's pattern of school enrollment most approximates that of the United States.

Enrollment in higher education, in Puerto Rico as elsewhere, is not uniformly open to the college-age population. The children of the middle class are more likely to attend college than those of the working class. Those who were born and raised in urban areas are more likely to be enrolled than those who were born and raised in the rural areas. However, sex is not a prominent factor in differential rates of enrollment, as it is in other countries. In Puerto Rico the number of males and females attending institutions of higher education is fairly comparable.

Why is Puerto Rico so dissimilar to other Latin American countries, as well as to other developing countries? Although the answer to this would require a study in itself, it is possible to speculate. As mentioned previously, education, particularly higher education, was neglected by the Spaniards during their rule in Puerto Rico. It was the United States, American educators, and in more recent years American-trained Puerto Ricans who built the Puerto Rican educational system. Its structure resembles that of the United States. It seems likely that the nature of the structure, in addition to the values infused into it and the society by the Americans, explains why the enrollment rates are so high for Puerto Rico. This point is further substantiated by the fact that the Philippines, a former possession of the United States, resembles Puerto Rico in its rates of enrollment in higher education. It may very well be that the Puerto Ricans have overconformed to the American value of rewarding according to achievement and to the American mean of achieving success through higher education.

Chapter III

NONUNIVERSITY SOURCES OF DIFFERENTIATION OF POLITICAL ATTITUDES
Family, Sex, Social Class, and Religion

By the time an adolescent enters a university, most of his values and attitudes have already been shaped. Entrance into an institution of higher learning does not erase the effects of such important determinants of values and behavior as family, sex, social class, and religion. It is therefore necessary to examine these factors and to ascertain their relationship to the political attitudes and behavior of the student. The factors that play upon the student at the university will be discussed later. This division should not imply that there are two distinct sets of variables with no interplay between them. The distinction between nonuniversity and university factors is only an analytical one.

FAMILY

The family molds the child's perception and expectations of the world around him. "The family is a key reference group which transmits, indoctrinates, and sustains the political loyalties of its members."[1] It is therefore reasonable to assume that Puerto Rican students are also the political children of their parents, particularly since in the Puerto Rican society there are very strong ties between parents and children.[2]

[1] Herbert McCloskey and Herbert E. Dahlgren, "Primary Group Influence in Party Loyalty," in *Politics in Social Life*, ed. Nelson W. Polsby, Robert A. Dentler, and Paul A. Smith, pp. 255–270.

[2] David Landy, *Tropical Childhood*; J. Mayone Stycos, *Family and Fertility in Puerto Rico*; and Melvin Tumin with Arnold Feldman, *Social Class and Social Change in Puerto Rico*.

Given the importance of the family, it seems pertinent to examine the influence of the student's family upon his politics. Studies of university students in different countries have demonstrated a relationship between students' residences and their political attitudes. Walker has noted that the pro-Castro Colombian student is likely to be the one who does not reside with his family.[3] Studies of Japanese, Indian, Chilean, and Parisian university students indicate that those students who live with their families are not as radical or as politically involved as those who live outside the home.[4] On the basis of these findings, we can assume that "living at home prolongs the authority of the family over the student and tends to insulate him from university influences."[5]

In order to test this hypothesis among the Puerto Rican students, the unmarried students were divided on the basis of whether or not they lived with their families, and the distribution of their responses to political items was compared. As Table 9 indicates, the distribution of political party preferences and political identities was similar for both groups. From this general comparison, whether a Puerto Rican student lives with his family or on his own seems to have little effect upon his political position.

[3] Kenneth N. Walker, "Determinants of Castro Support among Latin American University Students," *Social and Economic Studies*, 14, no. 1 (March, 1965) 100–101.

[4] Seymour M. Lipset, "University Students and Politics in Underdeveloped Countries," *Minerva*, 3, no. 1, (Autumn, 1964), 42–43. Professor Joseph Fischer says in private correspondence that this is not true of students he studied in Southeast Asia. Several studies of Berkeley students indicate that the relationship between living arrangements and political propensity is not uniformly consistent, even on the same campus. Selvin and Hagstrom have shown that the type of living arrangement, for the most part, has little effect upon whether or not a student is highly libertarian (Hannan Selvin and Warren O. Hagstrom, "Determinants of Support for Civil Liberties," *British Journal of Sociology*, 11 [March, 1960], 51–73). A study of Berkeley students who demonstrated in support of the Free Speech Movement indicated that the demonstrators were most likely to be apartment dwellers and least likely to be members of fraternities (Glen Lyons, "The Police Car Demonstration: A Survey of Participants," in *The Berkeley Student Revolt: Facts and Interpretations*, ed. Seymour M. Lipset and Sheldon S. Wolin, p. 521).

[5] Lipset, "University Students and Politics," p. 43.

TABLE 9

Influence of Residence on Student's Politics

	Residence	
Party Preference	Family %	Independent %
PIP	23	27
PPD	46	46
PER	29	23
PAC	2	4
Total	100	100
	=333	=143
Political Position	%	%
Left	21	22
Center	50	46
Right	29	32
Total	100	100
	=327	=139

However, when the political party preference of the father is introduced, the family does appear to insulate the student from outside political influences. Comparison of the politics of the home with the politics of the student now indicates the political directions in which students in different residence situations are likely to move. The data in Table 10 reveal that the pattern of residence does seem to make a difference, although the effects vary according to the political background of the home. Among those students who come from PIP backgrounds, residence with the family apparently inhibits outside political influences more than among students from other political backgrounds who live at home and more than among students from PIP families who live elsewhere. Residence patterns seem also to affect students from PER families, but not as noticeably as students from PIP homes. Among students from homes that can be considered rightist, living away from the family apparently frees the student to move toward the left. Among students from PPD families (who constitute the bulk of the students in the sample), residence patterns appear to have little independent impact.

It is necessary to point out that the data do not permit any state-

TABLE 10

Influence of Father's Party and Student's Residence on Student's Politics

	Father's Party					
	PIP		PPD		PER	
Student's	Student's Residence		Student's Residence		Student's Residence	
Party	Family	Independent	Family	Independent	Family	Independent
Preference	%	%	%	%	%	%
PIP	84	50	20	20	16	29
PPD	16	17	61	68	25	27
PER		33	16	9	59	42
PAC			2	3		2
Total	100	100	99*	100	100	100
	=25	=12	=201	=78	=107	=48

Student's Political Position	%	%	%	%	%	%
Left	59	17	17	21	17	24
Center	33	33	52	44	52	54
Right	8	50	32	35	31	22
Total	100	100	101*	100	100	100
	=27	=12	=192	=75	=103	=46

ment of uniform effect. The student who lives with a family that gives its allegiance to an almost extinct party is the most likely to resemble his family. Students from rightist families who live elsewhere appear to have differentiated themselves somewhat from their families. The nature of the residence of students whose families support the large centrist party does not appear to have much meaning. If residence pattern is an indication of parental influence, the extent to which it does have an effect varies according to the political background of the student.

There is, however, some reason to believe that the nature of residence may be a poor indicator of parental influence. The simple act of living in the same house does not necessarily mean that the student and his parents live in the same social world. Shared residence need not imply interaction and communication. Many of the radical activists who were interviewed did not seem to have been affected in their views or activities because they lived with their parents. Home for them was a place where they slept and occasionally ate meals. These students reported that they rarely spoke with their parents, although meaningful ties of affection still remained.[6]

All the FUPI activists interviewed stated that although they rarely discussed politics at home, their parents had in fact tried to curtail their political activities. However, the parents' opposition to their children's activities was very much secondary to their fear of FBI inquiries both at home and at their places of employment about their children's political activity. The students felt that the authorities were attempting to inhibit student leftist political activities by harassing the parents.

In order to explore further the nature of parental influence an attitudinal variable was introduced. The item used in this case was: "The most important thing a child should learn is to obey his parents." Although this item and the responses to it are probably imperfect indicators of the attitudes of the children toward their parents,[7] they may at least suggest how students feel about their parents. Negative responses to the question were interpreted to mean that the student was in the process of breaking away from his parents. If the responses were positive, the reverse would be true. Initially, it was hypothesized that persons who were breaking with their parents would be more likely to be leftist.[8] In the classic study of Bennington students by Theodore Newcombe, those who successfully resisted the liberalizing influence of the college community were also closely tied to or overly dependent upon their families.

---

[6] One of the more militant students interviewed was planning to move out of his parents' home because his mother objected to his late hours, his smoking, and his sloppy dress. He was quick to assure me, however, that whether he lived at home or not, he would always love his mother and intended to continue his financial assistance.

[7] The "obedience" item has been used in other studies as a measure of authoritarianism.

[8] Students were also asked the extent of their agreement with the item "When choosing a job one should arrange to work near his parents even if this means losing a good opportunity." The relationships of the responses to this item and the above political variables were very similar to those found for the "obedience" item.

The students who were most susceptible to change and who became more liberal were relatively independent of their families.[9]

The data in Table 11 are in accord with this hypothesis. Those who disagree most strongly with the statement are more likely to classify themselves as leftist and to choose the PIP than either those who moderately agree or those who strongly agree. In fact, there is a direct linear correlation between the extent of agreement and being leftist. That is, the more one disagrees with the statement, the more likely he is to be leftist and to prefer the PIP. Conversely, the more the student agrees with the item, the more likely he is to be rightist and to prefer the PER. When males and females were separated and their responses related to their political leanings, the data showed similar trends for each sex grouping. On the basis of these findings, it seems that students breaking with their parents in a society like Puerto Rico move to the left politically. This is some-

TABLE 11
Attitude toward Parents and Students' Politics

Responses to: "The most important thing a child should learn is to obey his parents."

Student's Party Preference	Strongly Agree %	Moderately Agree %	Disagree %
PIP	17	23	36
PPD	50	47	43
PER	31	27	19
PAC	2	3	2
Total	100	100	100
	=192	=225	=132
Student's Political Position	%	%	%
Left	16	18	35
Center	51	50	33
Right	33	32	32
Total	100	100	100
	=186	=222	=131

[9] Theodore M. Newcombe, *Personality and Social Change*, pp. 152–156.

what in line with what Edward Shils has described as the oppositional nature of the intellectuals.[10] It is also in accord with the
generational conflict school of thought.[11]

However, the data in Table 11 are not sufficient to support the
oppositional or generational conflict hypotheses. Do students with
leftist fathers move to the right? Do those students breaking away
from rightist parents move to the left? In order to answer these
questions, the political party of the father was introduced as a
third variable along with the obedience item and the politics of the
student. It then became possible to compare the percentage dis-
tributions of the students on the basis of their responses both to the
obedience question and to the political party preference of their
fathers.

As the data in Tables 12 and 13 indicate, there is some tendency
for the student breaking with his parents to move away from the
political position of his father. This is most clear in the case of
students from PER homes (see Table 13). As these students move
from strong agreement to disagreement, the percentage choosing
the PIP triples; those remaining loyal to the PER decline by twenty
percentage points. This tendency is not as evident in Table 12,
where relative political position is the dependent variable. However, among students from PER backgrounds, those who do not
agree that the most important thing a child should learn is to obey
his parents are most likely to be leftist. This is also true for students
from PPD families. In Table 13, among these same students, those
who disagree with the item are most likely to be supporters of the
PIP and least likely to prefer the PER. The situation is not as consistent when the children of PIP fathers are considered. In Table
12, those in this group who disagree are most likely to consider
themselves as rightist, but those who strongly agree are most likely
to consider themselves as leftist. In Table 13, students who moderately agree are least likely to support the PIP and most likely to

[10] Edward Shils, "The Intellectuals in the Political Development of the New
States," in *Political Change in Underdeveloped Countries: Nationalism and
Communism*, ed. John H. Kautsky, pp. 217, 229.

[11] See Lewis Feuer, *The Conflict of Generations*.

TABLE 12

Influence of Father's Party Preference and Student's Attitude toward Parents on Student's Political Position

Responses to: "The most important thing a child should learn is to obey his parents."

Student's Political Position	Father's Party Preference								
	PIP			PPD			PER		
	Strongly Agree %	Moderately Agree %	Disagree %	Strongly Agree %	Moderately Agree %	Disagree %	Strongly Agree %	Moderately Agree %	Disagree %
Left	58	26	54	12	18	36	15	15	29
Center	33	53	8	50	52	33	61	44	38
Right	8	21	38	38	30	31	24	41	33
Total	99*	100	100	100	100	100	100	100	100
	=12	=19	=13	=102	=127	=70	=59	=61	=42

TABLE 13

Influence of Father's Party Preference and Student's Attitude toward Parents on Student's Party Preference

Responses to: "The most important thing a child should learn is to obey his parents."

Student's Party Preference	Father's Party Preference								
	PIP			PPD			PER		
	Strongly Agree %	Moderately Agree %	Disagree %	Strongly Agree %	Moderately Agree %	Disagree %	Strongly Agree %	Moderately Agree %	Disagree %
PIP	82	56	79	15	19	30	11	22	33
PPD	18	22	14	67	62	61	26	25	21
PER		22	7	16	17	7	63	53	43
PAC				3	2	1			2
Total	100	100	100	101*	100	99*	100	100	99*

support the PER. Although the data are not thoroughly consistent, there does seem to be a general tendency for those who are breaking away from their parents to move in a political direction opposed to that of their fathers. Unfortunately, the evidence is least consistent among the children of leftist parents.

Traditionally, one of the better predictors of a person's politics has been the politics of the father.[12] McClosky and Dahlgren point out in their review of the literature that such primary groups as the family "are essential links in the complex process by which political norms are indoctrinated and party preferences implanted. . . . approximately three out of four young people vote as their parents do."[13] In our study the respondents identified the political party preference of their fathers; however, the father's politics may have changed over a period of time. If the students had been asked the nature of their fathers' politics while the students were in grammar school, the answer might possibly have been different, particularly for the independence-oriented parent. In interviews many leftist and rightist students said that their fathers had been in favor of independence during the thirties and early forties and then had changed, in the main to the PPD. Therefore it is not entirely clear that the father's current party preference is the one that has had the greatest impact upon the student. Another factor is that from the 1930's until 1948, a father who preferred independence could find no party on the ballot that openly espoused this position. Consequently, many such voters supported the independence wing of the PPD. In 1948, however, the PIP first appeared on the ballot. Possibly many supporters of independence maintained their allegiance to the PPD and never made the switch. However, with these shortcomings in mind, the data did tend to indicate a positive relationship between the political preferences of the fathers and those of their children, regardless of the party preference involved.

In Table 14 the fathers' political preferences were related to

[12] As in Herbert Hyman, *Political Socialization;* Paul F. Lazarsfeld, Bernard Berelson, and Harold Gaudet, *The People's Choice*, chapter 15; and McClosky and Dahlgren, "Primary Group Influence."

[13] McClosky and Dahlgren, "Primary Group Influence," pp. 255–256.

TABLE 14

Influence of Father's Party Preference on Student's Party Preference

Student's Party	Father's Party Preference			
Preference	PIP	PPD	PER	PAC
	%	%	%	%
PIP	70	19	20	22
PPD	19	65	25	22
PER	11	14	55	11
PAC	—	2	—	45
Total	100	100	100	100
	=43	=299	=170	=9†

† N is too small for percentages to be considered reliable.

TABLE 15

Influence of Fathers' Party Preference on Party Preference
of U.S. University Students

	"How does your father usually vote?"		
"Do you consider yourself in most matters:"	Republican	Democrat	Independent
	%	%	%
Republican	65	7	12
Democrat	4	52	12
Independent	29	39	75
Other	1	1	—
No Answer	1	1	—
Total	100	100	99*
	=1,025	=1,077	=412

From *What College Students Think*, by R. Goldsen, R. W. Williams, Jr., M. Rosenberg, and E. A. Suchman, Copyright © 1960 by Litton Educational Publishing, Inc., by permission of Van Nostrand Reinhold Company, p. 101.

those of the students. More than half of all the students had the same party preferences as their fathers. Fathers who supported the PIP were most likely to have sons follow in their political footsteps; 70 percent of these fathers had children who support the PIP. PPD fathers were almost as successful; 65 percent of this group had children who made the same political choice. A little more than half of the PER fathers had sons with the same political leanings. Thus the data indicate the power of political inheritance.

Fortunately, there are comparable data available on students in the United States. As seen in Table 15, American university students resembled their Puerto Rican counterparts in terms of political inheritance. Sixty-five percent of the Republican fathers had Republican children and 52 percent of the Democratic fathers had Democratic children. Also, a 1956 study of Boston University students reveals that over 70 percent of the respondents had the same political preference as their parents.[14] It is apparent that university students in two different political cultures—the United States, with a viable two-party system, and Puerto Rico, with one dominant party—tend to be influenced by the political choices of their fathers.

In order to obtain a different view of the political origins of the students, the data in Table 12 were turned around. Instead of asking what kinds of sons the fathers had produced, we asked where the children came from politically. Table 16 shows that almost 80 percent of the PPD students had PPD fathers, and about two-thirds of the PER students had fathers with PER preferences. However, only 24 percent of the PIP students had fathers with identical political affiliations. About one-half of the PIP students came from homes headed by fathers with PPD leanings; 27 percent had fathers who supported the PER. This reinforces the notion that PIP supporters

TABLE 16
Student's Party Preference by Father's Party

Father's Party	Student's Party Preference			
	PIP %	PPD %	PER %	PAC %
PIP	24	3	3	—
PPD	47	79	30	50
PER	27	17	66	10
PAC	2	1	1	40
Total	100	100	100	100
	=124	=245	=142	=10†

† N is too small for percentages to be considered reliable.

14 Phillip Nogee and Marvin B. Levin, "Some Determinants of Political Attitudes among College Voters," *Public Opinion Quarterly*, 22, no. 4 (Winter, 1958), 455–456. Hyman summarizes studies of the 1920's and 1930's which show that college students then also tended to follow their fathers' political choice (Hyman, *Political Socialization*, pp. 139–150).

TABLE 17

Influence of Father's Party on Student's Political Position

| Student's Political Position | Father's Party | | | |
	PIP %	PPD %	PER %	PAC %
Left	43	20	19	30
Center	34	47	49	40
Right	23	33	32	30
Total	100	100	100	100
	=44	=289	=164	=10†

† N is too small for percentages to be considered reliable.

are more likely to be political and family mavericks than either PPD or PER students.

One can assume that, to a certain extent, the party preference of the father reflects a left, center, or right position (PIP, PPD, and PER respectively). If this is true, it is interesting to note the influence of the father's party preference upon the student's ideological position (left, center, right) relative to that of other students. In Table 17 we see that PIP fathers, compared with PPD and PER fathers, produced more children who considered themselves leftist and fewer who considered themselves rightist. In fact, students with PIP fathers were more than twice as likely to identify themselves as leftists than students with PPD or PER fathers. The students' relative political positions do not seem to have been affected by whether the father preferred the PPD or PER; the distribution is virtually identical in both cases. This might reflect the growing similarity between the PER and the PPD parties.

The data offered support the contention that the family and attitudes toward it are major determinants in the formation of the politics of students, indicating (1) that the party preferences of the students and their fathers are far more similar than dissimilar, and (2) that leftists and activists are more likely than other students to be in the process of pulling away from the influence of their parents.

SEX AND POLITICS

As 43 percent of the sample is female, the often neglected variable of sex should be considered, in order to see if political differences among the Puerto Rican students might be in some way affected by sex. According to evidence from studies around the world, women are less involved politically and less liberal than men. Social scientists believe that this stems primarily from the social role of women that ties them to the home and removes them from the concern of things outside the home.[15] These political differences between the sexes have been found even among grammar school students.[16] A study of students at the National University in Colombia indicates that the female students differed politically from their male counterparts. "Political indifference, ignorance, and conservatism were decidedly observable on the part of the female students."[17] With these findings in mind, male and female students at the University of Puerto Rico were compared on the basis of their political positions and activities. It was expected that the Puerto Rican females would resemble their counterparts elsewhere, that they too would be more conservative and less likely to participate actively in politics than the male students. Our findings did, in fact, conform somewhat with these expectations.

About 45 percent of the males, compared with 29 percent of the females, thought themselves to be more leftist than other students. However, there is virtually no difference between the percentage of males and females who consider themselves rightist (see Table 18). Coeds are also more likely to assume the safe political position of the center: 57 percent (females) versus 41 percent (males). In

[15] Fred Greenstein, "Sex Related Political Differences in Childhood," in *Politics in Social Life*, ed. Polsby, Dentler, and Smith, p. 245; Robert Lane, *Political Life*, pp. 209–216; Hyman, *Political Socialization*, pp. 29–35; Seymour M. Lipset, *Political Man*, pp. 187, 231; and Gabriel Almand and Sidney Verba, *Civic Culture*, pp. 324–335.

[16] Greenstein, "Sex Related Political Differences," p. 247; and Hyman, *Political Socialization*, pp. 29–35.

[17] Robert C. Williamson, *El estudiante colombiano y sus actitudes*, p. 73.

TABLE 18
Influence of Sex on Political Position

Political Position	Male %	Female %
Left	45	30
Center	41	57
Right	14	13
Total	100	100
	=291	=219

terms of political party preference, the overall difference between the percentages of males and females who support each party was not large. The greatest differences occurred between males and females who preferred the PIP; in this case, 29 percent of the men, compared with 19 percent of the women, supported the PIP. A study done almost ten years earlier at the University of Puerto Rico reports similar differences in male and female support for the PIP.[18] On other political indicators of liberalism and conservatism, the males were more likely than the females to favor government intervention in the economy, equal distribution of income, Castro, and easing of divorce restrictions.

When the sexes were compared as to political activity, males were more active both in voting and in demonstrating. About 45 percent (304) of the males compared with about 30 percent (223) of the females, voted in the last school election. Twenty-eight percent (319) of the males claimed to have participated in demonstrations, contrasted with 12 percent (239) of the females.

In order to ascertain the effects of both sex and relative political position, these two variables were related simultaneously to other political items. The data in Table 19 show that males and females within each category (left, center, and right) are more alike than their sexual counterparts who take different political stances. This is vividly illustrated in support for the PIP. The percentage differ-

18 Peter Bachrach, "Attitude toward Authority and Party Preference in Puerto Rico," *Public Opinion Quarterly*, 22 (1958), p. 72.

ence between females and males who are leftist and support the PIP is less than 2 percent. The difference between males and females who described themselves as rightist and also support the PIP is about 7 percent. When the sexes were compared on the basis of their responses concerning the distribution of incomes and the position of the government in the economy, sex continued to play a subordinate role to political position. Once again, females within each political category more resembled the males in that category than other females. Although sex does appear to have political relevance, its importance declines after political identification has been made.

In general, the findings reveal that, as expected, females are less likely to be leftist and less likely to be politically active than males. The differences, however, are not large. This particular finding is supported by other studies that consider political differences between the sexes and take account of the educational level of the men and women. In *The American Voter*, the authors have found that both voting rates and feelings of political efficacy increase among women as their education increases.[19] Robert Lane supports the contention about voting, pointing to the fact that the voting turnout among the middle class is higher and more equally divided between the sexes than it is among the working class.[20] In Almond and Verba's five-nation study, political participation, obligation, and competence of women increase as their education increases. This is true for all five nations—Germany, Italy, Mexico, Britain, and the United States.[21] The more educated the woman, the more likely she is to deviate from the traditional status and role given to her by society. Education is perhaps a liberating and an egalitarianizing experience. As far as the Puerto Rican students are concerned, political differences among the students at the University of Puerto Rico do not appear to stem significantly from sex differences.

[19] Angus Campbell *et al.*, *The American Voter*, pp. 257–258.
[20] Lane, *Political Life*, p. 214.
[21] Almond and Verba, *Civic Culture*, pp. 329–333.

TABLE 19
Influence of Sex on Relative Political Position and Party Preference

	Political Position					
	Left		Center		Right	
Party	Male	Female	Male	Female	Male	Female
Preference	%	%	%	%	%	%
PIP	68	67	17	13	13	6
PPD	25	22	50	54	54	57
PER	4	11	31	30	32	34
PAC	3	—	2	3	1	3
Total	100	100	100	100	100	100
	=76	=36	=127	=121	=100	=70

SOCIAL CLASS

The social class origins of the students can affect their political outlook and activities. However, the literature makes clear that there is no simple relationship between the class and the politics of university students. For example, two contrasting effects of similar social class can be hypothesized. Students from lower-status families might be more likely to be conservative, since for them the university is purely a means for social mobility. On the other hand, students from lower-class families might be more likely to be radical because of social rejection at the university. In specifying the influence of class on student politics, the social-class characteristics of the environing society must also be taken into account. Students from disadvantaged homes have different social experiences, determined by the extent to which their society is class conscious. Bonilla asserts that the leadership of student politics in Chile came from socially disadvantaged groups who were deeply aware of their origins because of the high degree of class consciousness in that country.[22] Lipset cites studies from a number of countries that illustrate how social class can affect student politics; in most cases

[22] Frank Bonilla, "Students in Politics: Three Generations of Political Action in a Latin American University," Ph.D. dissertation, Harvard University, 1959, p. 253.

the lower-status groups tend more than others to be politically active and radical.[23] A study of eleven universities in the United States has found a strong positive correlation between family income and party preference; the poorer the student's family, the more likely he is to prefer the Democratic party (traditionally, the more liberal one).[24] Reviewing data from Antioch, Reed, Swarthmore, San Francisco State, and the University of California at Berkeley, Professors Martin Trow and Burton Clark note that "the effects of selective recruitment (through both self-recruitment and admissions screening) along lines of academic orientations and aptitudes are so strong that they wash out, or at least greatly reduce, differences in cultural and intellectual orientations that stem from differences in social origins among students within any one of these colleges."[25]

However, there are indications that social class may not be an important determinant of student political behavior. After finding that Colombian university students' attitudes toward Castro did not differ greatly by social class, Walker suggests "that either the political orientation of students' families does not vary much by social strata, or else the students do not reflect the political cleavages that may exist in the larger society."[26] Walker goes on to say that this might be a result of age homogeneity, the common social status of student, and the shared university experience.[27]

Because of Puerto Rico's emphasis upon mass education at even the higher levels, the island's university population is drawn from a wide social base. In other parts of Latin America the university students are more homogeneous in terms of class. One could hypothesize that, because of this heterogeneity, social class might prove to be a more influential factor among Puerto Rican university students than among other Latin American students. The importance of class as a differential determinant of social behavior

[23] Lipset, "University Students and Politics," pp. 47–48.
[24] Rose K. Goldsen *et al.*, *What College Students Think*, p. 103.
[25] Martin Trow and Burton Clark, "The Organizational Context," in *College Peer Groups*, ed. Theodore M. Newcombe and E. K. Wilson, pp. 29–30.
[26] Walker, "Determinants of Castro Support," p. 99.
[27] *Ibid.*

TABLE 20
Influence of Father's Education on Student's Politics

| Student's Political Position | Father's Education | | |
	University %	Secondary School %	Elementary School %
Left	23	21	18
Center	47	48	42
Right	30	31	40
Total	100	100	100
	=113	=247	=178

within a student body would seem greater among students with sizable representations from different segments of society than on a campus characterized by relative class homogeneity.

In order to determine class effects, three separate indicators of class were used, the education of the father,[28] the occupation of the father, and the student's own assessment of his family's class. Each of these variables was then related to the student's ideological position and party preference. The data reveal that, regardless of the indicator of social class employed, social class has little effect upon the politics of Puerto Rican university students. As seen in Table 20, the percentage of the students whose fathers had an elementary school education and who considered themselves leftist was 18 percent, compared with 23 percent of those with university-educated fathers. In general, Table 20 shows a great similarity in the responses of the students, regardless of the parental educational level. However, those students most likely to identify themselves as rightist are those whose fathers had the least education. When the fathers' occupation was used (see Table 21), similar trends were noted. Once again, the greatest identification with the right was among the lowest status group. When subjective class was con-

[28] In Tumin's study of social class in Puerto Rico, education was used as the major indicator and provided a fairly good picture of a person's position on the criteria of property, prestige, and power (Tumin, *Social Class and Social Change*, p. 44).

sidered (see Table 22), there were few differences among the social class groupings. Twenty-one percent of those identifying themselves as upper class felt they were leftist, contrasted with 26 percent of those identifying themselves as lower class.

The student's social class as measured by each of the three indicators was also related to his political party preference. The social background of the student had little bearing upon party preference. Table 23 indicates that there was no correlation between the education of the father and the student's preference for either the

TABLE 21
Influence of Father's Occupational Level on Student's Politics

Student's Political Position	Father's Occupational Level†			
	Upper %	Middle %	Minor %	Lower %
Left	26	20	21	16
Center	42	51	46	44
Right	32	29	33	40
Total	100	100	100	100
	=158	=175	=95	=83

† Upper: Proprietor with 21 or more persons occupied; university-trained professional with high level of training; high official (with 100 or more persons under orders)
Middle: Proprietor with 11–20 persons occupied; university-trained professional with low level of training; minor and intermediate official
Minor: Proprietor with less than 11 persons occupied; clerical worker
Lower: Blue-collar worker

TABLE 22
Subjective Social Class and Student's Political Position

Student's Political Position	Subjective Social Class		
	Upper %	Middle %	Lower %
Left	21	20	26
Center	44	51	46
Right	35	30	28
Total	100	101*	100
	=260	=173	=88

TABLE 23
Influence of Father's Education on Student's Party Preference

| | Father's Education | | |
Student's Party Preference	University %	Secondary School %	Elementary School %
PIP	20	25	25
PPD	46	27	48
PER	32	47	22
PAC	2	1	5
Total	100	100	100
	=183	=240	=108

TABLE 24
Influence of Father's Occupational Level on Student's Party Preference

| Student's Party Preference | Father's Occupational Level | | | |
	Upper %	Middle %	Minor %	Lower %
PIP	27	23	22	21
PPD	38	50	55	54
PER	33	27	21	22
PAC	2	—	2	3
Total	100	100	100	100
	=158	=104	=98	=82

PIP or the PPD. The correlation between father's education and support for the PER is not a linear one. Students whose fathers had a secondary school education were most likely to prefer the PER, whereas those whose fathers had only an elementary school education were the least likely to favor this party. In Table 24, the father's occupation had little bearing upon party preference, except again in the case of the PER. Although the trend in terms of support for the PER is not as consistent when the father's education is used, the range remains similar. When subjective class is used as an indicator (see Table 25), the data reveal that subjective class has little relationship to party preferences. There is a slight positive

TABLE 25
Subjective Social Class and Student's Party Preference

Student's Party Preference	Subjective Social Class		
	Upper %	Middle %	Lower %
PIP	25	22	25
PPD	43	50	50
PER	31	25	21
PAC	1	3	4
Total	100	100	100
	=265	=175	=91

correlation between subjective class and support for the PER, but again the difference is not large.

Contrary to our original expectation, social class is not a major determinant of Puerto Rican student politics. However, there are aspects of Puerto Rican society that might explain this finding. Tumin's study of social class in Puerto Rico indicates that class is not a major differentiating factor among the Puerto Rican people.[29] This lack of a class conflict is evident in the weakness of the Puerto Rican labor movement. Traditional paternalistic relations between workers and employers are still found in Puerto Rico. "Workers commonly identify with the employer as a person and desire a recognition directly from him."[30] On the basis of his study of social class in Puerto Rico, Tumin asserts:

There is very high morale in all segments of the Puerto Rican community. The present inequalities are not perceived as insuperable obstacles. The social order is viewed at all levels of the class structure as a fair and reasonable arrangement. Members of all classes feel well integrated and feel it is worth giving their loyalty to the society and their effort toward its development. In these terms, though they are decidedly unequally equipped with the required skills, people at all

[29] Tumin, *Social Class and Social Change*, pp. 164–184.
[30] Lloyd G. Reynolds and Peter Gregory, *Wages, Productivity, and Industrialization in Puerto Rico*, p. 287.

levels are relatively equally equipped for the future with the spirit required.[31]

This lack of class consciousness may be reflected in the political attitudes of Puerto Rican university students.

RELIGION

It has been estimated that Roman Catholicism is the religion of about 85 percent of the Puerto Rican population.[32] As in many other Latin American countries, however, there is some doubt as to the degree of commitment to the Catholic religion itself, as well as to the Church.[33] For many Puerto Ricans today, Catholicism is a mixture of spiritualism, saints, and ceremonies, rather than a conscious religious creed. For the lower class especially, Catholicism is in many ways hardly distinguishable from magic. Large numbers of Puerto Ricans neither attend Mass, obtain sacraments, go to confession, nor have their marriages performed by the Church. Also, the Church's position regarding birth control is not rigidly adhered to by the populace.[34] In Tumin's study, almost four out of every ten respondents reported that they never attended church, while another 34 percent claimed that they went less than once a week.[35]

The causes of the Church's lack of influence are manifold. During Puerto Rico's Spanish era, the Church was successful in preventing non-Catholics from entering the island. This pretwentieth-century success has contributed a great deal to the contemporary difficulties of the Church. Since the Church did not have to compete for the support of the people, it became lax in seeking to establish meaningful ties with them.[36] Another difficulty faced by the

[31] Tumin, *Social Class and Social Change*, pp. 164–165.

[32] *National Catholic Almanac 1965*, p. 235.

[33] Theodore Brameld, *The Remaking of a Culture*, p. 105; Stycos, *Family and Fertility*, p. 198; Gordon K. Lewis, *Puerto Rico: Freedom and Power in the Caribbean*, pp. 271–280.

[34] J. H. Steward *et al.*, eds., *The People of Puerto Rico*, pp. 42, 85, 128; Landy, *Tropical Childhood*, p. 41; Stycos, *Family and Fertility*, pp. 198–199.

[35] Tumin, *Social Class and Social Change*, p. 281.

[36] Steward *et al.*, eds., *People of Puerto Rico*, p. 42.

contemporary Church was, and to some extent still is, the failure of the Church to recruit a native clergy. It is claimed that if all the non–Puerto Rican clergy were to be expelled from the island, only seventy clergy would remain.[37] Until the 1960's, Puerto Rico had no native-born bishop.[38]

Added to these problems is the shortage of priests, native or foreign born, on the island. There is approximately one priest for every 7,000 Catholics in Puerto Rico.[39] In the United States there is about one priest for every 2,500 Catholics; in Chile, one for every 2,700; in Mexico, one for every 4,800.[40] In actuality the per capita figures, at least for Puerto Rico, are somewhat misleading, since the clergy is not proportionately distributed throughout the island. There seems to be a greater scarcity of priests in the countryside than in the cities. According to recent study of a Puerto Rican village, the villagers claimed that they had not seen a priest or been inside a church for many years.[41]

A Puerto Rican church that was not very Puerto Rican and that lacked sufficient clerics was not likely as an institution to establish widespread influence on the island. In addition, the Church's traditionally conservative stance has served to weaken its support among the populace. Even after the infusion of American clergy, the Puerto Rican church has remained a predominantly conservative institution. One historical example of its conservatism was the failure of the Catholic hierarchy in Puerto Rico to take an antislavery position like that taken by the Vatican. Not only did the Puerto Rican church defend slavery, but it also owned its own slaves.[42] Further contributing to the Church's weakened support among the masses has been its traditional alliance with the upper and middle classes. This is evident from the various Protestant inroads among

[37] Lewis, *Freedom and Power*, p. 277.

[38] Robert Anderson, *Party Politics in Puerto Rico*, p. 231.

[39] Nathan Glazer and Daniel P. Moynihan, *Beyond the Melting Pot: The Ethnic Groups of New York City*, p. 88.

[40] Center of Latin American Studies, *Statistical Abstract of Latin America 1963*, p. 33.

[41] Landy, *Tropical Childhood*, p. 42.

[42] Steward *et al.*, eds., *People of Puerto Rico*, pp. 42–43.

the Puerto Rican lower class. In 1942 it was estimated that more than two-thirds of the members of the evangelical Protestant churches earned less than $300 a year.[43] Moreover, the conservative nature of the Church has led it to oppose the PPD and its various reforms. In a statement written in 1952, the Roman Catholic Bishop of Ponce declared:

The Popular Party has been an enemy of Catholic ideals for many years; the leaders of that party, lacking religious convictions, have given too much importance to their economic convictions, forgetting Christ's teaching that man does not live by bread alone. . . . The policy of the Popular Party has been so contrary to Catholic life that the Bishop should have advised Catholics not to vote for the Popular Party. . . . If our words have been in vain and the election results confirm the belief of the political leaders that religion does not influence the vote . . . then it is to be expected that the Popular Party will continue its amoral policies.[44]

This attitude led the Church hierarchy to form its own party in 1960—the Christian Action Party. In its first showings at the polls in 1960, this party drew 7 percent of the vote.[45] In the same election the Church had made opposition to the PPD a matter of religious obligation and had charged the PPD as openly attacking religion. Despite this strong stand by the Church, the PPD received 58 percent of the vote in that election. In the 1964 election, the Christian Action Party's share of the vote dropped to 3 percent.[46] Support for the Church-backed party was even less among the university students. In our sample, only thirteen, or 2 percent of the entire sample, voiced preference for this party.

The formation of a religious party and open hostility by the Church toward the Populares represent a break with tradition. Until this time there had been no attempt by the Church to align the religiously faithful within the confines of one party. The failure

---

[43] *Ibid.*, p. 87. It should be remembered that in a society whose population is about 85 percent Catholic, the majority of all classes is Catholic.

[44] Quoted in Anderson, *Party Politics*, pp. 215–216.

[45] *Ibid.*, p. 216.

[46] *Ibid.*, p. 112; and Lewis, *Freedom and Power*, p. 279.

of this attempt to receive mass backing for a clerical party bears testimony to the Church's weak political position in Puerto Rico. The Church was unable to change the reality that not only does each of the major political parties include large numbers of Catholics, but religious affiliation has not been a factor in party identification.[47]

The dispersal of the religiously faithful throughout the various parties is to some extent associated with the fact that the Church has not taken a clear stand on the status issue. One can be a good Catholic and favor either independence, statehood, or commonwealth status for Puerto Rico. The status issue, however, has had the effect of throwing together some ardent Catholics with some of the so-called radical elements favoring independence. These Catholics desire an independent Puerto Rico in order to maintain the religious purity of a truly Catholic Puerto Rico. In their view, only a politically independent Puerto Rico could successfully resist the encroachments of Anglo-Saxon Protestant materialism.[48]

There is some indication that this Catholic grouping may have fallen into disfavor with the Catholic hierarchy in recent years. Several student respondents have claimed that Father Marguerito, a leader of the proindependence organization Crusadio Patriótica Cristiana, has been chastized by the bishops because of his proindependence activities.[49]

The Catholic Church has been unable to influence the political behavior of the Puerto Rican populace. Although in other Latin American countries Church-supported parties have achieved mass support, the Puerto Rican church has been quite unsuccessful in its political endeavors.

Religiosity of Puerto Rican Students

Although the Church may be unable seriously to influence political behavior, there is some indication that religion does have a

[47] Anderson, *Party Politics*, p. 112; and Lewis, *Freedom and Power*, p. 278.
[48] Lewis, *Freedom and Power*, p. 278.
[49] From unpublished interviews with University of Puerto Rico students, summer, 1965.

TABLE 26
*Frequency of Church Attendance by University Students
in Puerto Rico, Mexico, and the United States*

Church Attendance	Puerto Rico %	Mexico %	United States %
Once a week or more	54	49	27
Never and almost never	21	29	25
Total†	75	78	52
	=567	=802	=2,975

† Totals do not equal 100 as only extreme categories of church attendance were used.

certain influence on student political behavior. It is therefore necessary to examine the students' religiosity and the relationship between it and politics.

If frequency of church attendance is used as an indicator of religiosity, there are data available to illustrate that Puerto Rican students are more religious than their counterparts in Mexico and in the United States. Table 26 compares university students in Mexico, Puerto Rico, and the United States on the basis of their frequency of church attendance. Attendance by Puerto Rican students at the level of once a week or more is slightly higher than attendance by Mexican students and more than twice as high as attendance by students in the United States, who are much more likely than the Puerto Ricans to be Protestant and therefore have less pressure for regular weekly attendance. Puerto Rican students are least likely to be found among those who never attend church.

Several other indicators of religiosity reveal Mexican students more likely than Puerto Rican students to identify themselves as nonpracticing Catholics, atheists, and agnostics. When asked to classify themselves according to their own conception of religiosity, 79 percent of the Puerto Rican students replied "very" or "moderately" religious, compared with 54 percent of the Mexican students.

It might also be instructive to compare Puerto Rican students with Puerto Rican adults in terms of religiosity. Once again, in terms of church attendance, Puerto Rican students seem much

TABLE 27

Frequency of Church Attendance by Adults† and University Students

Church Attendance	Puerto Rican Students %	13+ Years of Education %	Adults (ca. .75 male) Main Sample %	Adults (ca. .75 female) Spouses %
Once a week or more	54	51	29	29
Less than once a week	37	31	34	33
Never	9	18	37	38
Total	100 =567	100 =71	100 =994	100 =782

† Source for adults is Tumin, *Social Class and Social Change*, pp. 281–282.

more religious than Puerto Rican adults. As seen in Table 27, 54 percent of the Puerto Rican students attend church once a week or more, but only about 29 percent of the adults attend as frequently. Interestingly enough, the figure for the adults is approximately the same whether predominantly male or predominantly female samples are used. Also, only 9 percent of the students claim they never attend church; the percentage for the adults is four times as high. However, it may not be fair to compare university students with the sample of adults from the entire population. Fortunately, it is possible to compare students' religious attendance with that of university-educated adults. When this is done, the differences are dramatically reduced; 50 percent of the university-educated adults claim they attend church once a week or more. The percentage of adults never attending drops to 18 percent. However, students still seem slightly more religiously inclined than even this group. Melvin Tumin found in his study that there was a tendency among adults for church attendance to increase as years of education increased.[50]

The students were compared among themselves as to religiosity.

[50] Tumin, *Social Class and Social Change*, pp. 281–289.

TABLE 28

Influence of Father's Education on Frequency of Student's Church Attendance

Student's Church Attendance	Father's Education		
	Elementary %	Secondary %	University %
Never	27	22	21
1–2 times a month	15	29	22
More than 2 times a month	58	49	58
Total	100 =113	100 =247	101* =187

TABLE 29

Influence of Mother's Religion on Student's Self-defined Religiosity

Student's Religiosity	Mother's Religion			
	Practicing Catholic %	Other Religion %	Nonpracticing Catholic %	Not Religious; Atheist, Agnostic %
Religious	87	80	72	53
Nonreligious	13	19	28	48
Total	100 =252	99* =155	100 =113	101* = 19

In order to ascertain whether background variables affected the religiosity of the students, social status, sex, and the mother's religious background were related to the religiosity of the student. When the social status of the student as measured by his father's education was related to the religiosity of the student, the data as shown in Table 28 indicate that social status does not meaningfully differentiate the religious from the nonreligious student. Social status, it would seem, has little impact upon either the religiosity or the politics of the students who reach the university.

In Table 29, the religious background of the student's mother was related to his own religiosity. It was hypothesized that the mother's religious background would have a direct relationship with the religiosity of her child. In the division of labor between male and female, the female is the sociointegrative leader, and in Latin Catholic lands she more than the male attends services and is the most concerned with religion. The data in Table 29 support the hypothesis: almost 90 percent of the students whose mothers are practicing Catholics consider themselves to be religious; almost half of those whose mothers are nonreligious feel themselves to be nonreligious. This is telling testimony to the influence of the mother in the religious sphere.

Next, males and females were compared on the basis of their religiosity. On several indicators the females were more religious than the males. As seen in Table 30, 34 percent of the males declared themselves to be practicing Catholics, compared with 65 percent of the females. Among nonpracticing Catholics and nonreligious students, the males predominate. Moreover, 91 percent of the females consider themselves to be religious, compared with 72 percent of the males. It seems safe to conclude that religion is a meaningful factor for the Puerto Rican student body and that it has a greater impact on the females than on the males.

TABLE 30
Student's Religion and Sex

Student's Religious Affiliation	Male %	Female %
Practicing Catholic	34	65
Other	14	14
Nonpracticing Catholic	35	15
Nonreligious	16	6
Total	101*	100
	=323	=244
Student's Self-defined Religiosity	%	%
Religious	72	91
Nonreligious	28	9
Total	100	100
	=325	=242

TABLE 31
Influence of Religion on Party Preference

Political Party	Practicing Catholic %	Other Religion %	Nonpracticing Catholic %	Not Religious %
PIP	17	20	27	53
PPD	49	60	48	35
PER	34	20	25	12
Total	100	100	100	100
	=248	=76	=143	=66

TABLE 32
Religion and Political Position

Political Position	Practicing Catholic %	Other Religion %	Nonpracticing Catholic %	Not Religious %
Left	14	15	24	52
Center	51	49	48	22
Right	36	37	28	26
Total	101*	101*	100	100
	=258	=75	=138	=69

Religion and Politics

What implications does this finding have on the politics of the students? In order to answer this question, indicators of religiosity and political preference were interrelated. As Table 31 shows, with the movement from "practicing Catholic," to "other religion," to "nonpracticing Catholic," and finally to "nonreligious," preference for the PIP progressively increases from 17 percent in the case of practicing Catholics to 53 percent in the case of nonreligious students. Also, practicing Catholics are most likely to support the Republican Statehood party (34%), whereas the nonreligious are least likely to do so (12%). When the same religious groupings were compared as to their preferences for the solution of the political status issue, a similar pattern unfolded.

In Table 32 the same religious groupings were compared as to their political position vis-à-vis other students. Again, as one moves from "practicing Catholic" to "nonreligious," the percentage of students claiming to be leftist increases from 14 percent to 52 percent. Those students who claim to be practicing their religion are more likely than the nonpracticing Catholics and the nonreligious Catholics to be rightist. Other indicators of religiosity reveal similar tendencies. Those who rarely or never attend church are more likely than their more conscientious peers to be leftist, while those who attended church more than twice a month are more likely to be rightist (see Table 33). When those students who consider themselves religious were compared with those who do not, the nonreligious students were more leftist. As seen in Table 34, 38 percent of the nonreligious students responded leftist, compared with 17 percent of the religious students. Conversely, 35 percent of the

TABLE 33
Church Attendance and Political Position

Political Position	Never and Almost Never %	1–2 Times per Month %	More than Twice per Month %
Left	38	26	13
Center	38	45	50
Right	25	29	37
Total	101* =112	100 =129	100 =296

TABLE 34
Religious Self-Image and Political Position

	Self-Image	
Political Position	Religious %	Nonreligious %
Left	17	38
Center	48	38
Right	35	24
Total	100 =437	100 =107

religious students, compared with 24 percent of the nonreligious students, answered rightist.

Lenski and Stouffer have both pointed to the fact that the more involved a person is in his religion, the less likely he is to be liberal in a variety of areas. Since the Roman Catholic Church in Puerto Rico is a predominantly conservative institution, especially in the political sense, one would expect that those Puerto Ricans most highly involved in it to be in some ways affected by its conservative stance.[51]

The religious groupings were also compared by their attitudes toward the reduction of income differentials and the easing of divorce restrictions. Such comparisons showed a tendency for the less religious to be more liberal in social and economic areas than the more religious. These findings conform with other studies. Kenneth Walker has shown that, in the case of Colombian university students, support for Castro was greater among the nonreligious than among the religious. This support for Castro was also directly related to frequency of church attendance; the less one attended, the more likely he was to be pro-Castro.[52] Studies of American university students also support the notion that the less religiously involved or committed a student is, the more likely he is to be liberal in different areas.[53] A study of Berkeley students dealing specifically with the issue of libertarianism has shown that those students who do not attend church are more likely to be highly libertarian than those who do. Studies of adults in the United States and other countries show that the nonchurchgoer is more likely to be liberal or leftist than the churchgoer.[54]

[51] Gerhard Lenski, *The Religious Factor*, pp. 175 and 191; Samuel A. Stouffer, *Communism, Conformity, and Civil Liberties*, pp. 145–151. When our respondents were asked the extent to which they agreed or disagreed with the statement that "the only way to understand our present confused world is to listen to the leaders and other trustworthy persons," a positive correlation was found between those who agreed and those who were practicing Catholics. Thus, the further away the respondent was from being a practicing Catholic, the more likely he was to disagree with the statement.

[52] Walker, "Determinants of Castro Support," p. 98.

[53] Goldsen *et al.*, *What College Students Think*, pp. 169–195.

[54] Charles Y. Glock and Rodney Stark, *Religion and Society in Tension*, pp.

TABLE 35
Influence of Religious Self-Image and Sex on Student's Politics

| | Male | | Female | |
| | Religious | Nonreligious | Religious | Nonreligious |
Relative Political Position	%	%	%	%
Left	21	36	13	48
Center	43	37	54	43
Right	36	27	33	9
Total	100	100	100	100
	=224	=86	=213	=21
Student's Party Preference	%	%	%	%
PIP	25	36	17	35
PPD	43	48	51	50
PER	29	15	29	15
PAC	3	1	3	—
Total	100	100	100	100
	=228	=89	=214	=20

The question might be raised as to whether this relationship between religiosity and politics might be a function of sex. As mentioned earlier, females are likely to be more religious than males, and therefore the findings might indicate a sex difference and not a religious one. This does not seem to be the case (see Table 35). When sex is controlled for, the nonreligious within each sex grouping are more likely to be leftist than are the religious. Conversely, the religious student, regardless of sex, is more likely than the nonreligious student to be rightist. When the comparisons are made in terms of political party preferences, the male and female nonreligious students are more likely than their religious counterparts to prefer the PIP. The religious student, regardless of sex, is more likely than the nonreligious of either sex to prefer the PER. In fact, the percentage of students supporting each political party is virtual-

201–226; and Stouffer, *Communism, Conformity, and Civil Liberties,* pp. 140–152.

TABLE 36

Year Entered University and Religious Affiliation

Religious Affiliation	After 1961		Before 1961	
	M %	F %	M %	F %
Practicing Catholic	43	71	28	54
Other religion	11	14	15	15
Nonpracticing Catholic	33	12	37	20
Not religious	13	3	20	11
Total	100	100	100	100
	=125	=157	=198	=87

ly identical for nonreligious male and female students and generally similar for the religious male and female students.

The University Experience

Up to this point, preuniversity background variables have been considered. It would be instructive, however, to examine too the way in which the university experience affects the relationship between religion and politics.[55] In order to ascertain this, students were divided between those who enrolled before and those who enrolled after 1961, as well as on the basis of whether or not their religiosity had undergone any change since they entered the university. Table 36 indicates that those who have been in school longer have become less religious. This is true for both males and females. The percentage of practicing Catholic females declined from 71 percent to 54 percent; nonreligious females increased from 2 percent to 11 percent. For the males, the corresponding figures were 43 percent to 28 percent for practicing Catholics, and 13 percent to 20 percent for the nonreligious.

Since this is not panel data, one could argue that the shift in religiosity might represent a disproportionate dropout of the more

[55] The discussion here will be brief, since the impact of the university experience is considered in greater detail elsewhere.

religious students; that is, the more religious students more than the nonreligious tend to leave school. In order to address this issue, the students were divided according to the date they entered school and then compared as to whether or not they reported a change in their religious sentiments since entering school. As seen in Table 37, students who have been in school longer report more change in their religiosity than the other students. The direction of the change, however, is more relevant. Both groups of students are more likely to become "less" than "more" religious. However, thirty-one percent of those who entered before 1961, compared with 12 percent of those who entered after 1961, reported that they had become less religious. In the absence of panel data, the available evidence indicates that the longer the individual remains in school, the less religious he becomes.

The political effects of this lessening of religiosity can be seen in Table 38. Those students who became less religious were more likely than those who became more religious or experienced no religious change to consider themselves leftist. The students who became more religious were more likely to consider themselves rightist. When the students were compared on political party affiliation, those who became less religious were more likely to support the PIP. Not only does religiosity undergo a change through the university experience, but that change seems to be reflected in political inclination as well.

TABLE 37
Change in Religious Sentiment since Entering College

Change in Religious Sentiment	Length of Time in School	
	After 1961 %	Before 1961 %
As religious	82	55
More religious	6	14
Less religious	12	31
Total	100	100
	=282	=283

TABLE 38
Political Position and Change in Religious Sentiment since Entering College

Political Position	As Religious %	More Religious %	Less Religious %
Left	17	21	39
Center	49	38	41
Right	34	41	20
Total	100	100	100
	=352	=51	=111
Party Preference	%	%	%
PIP	19	30	37
PPD	49	50	37
PER	31	13	24
PAC	1	7	2
Total	100	100	100
	=358	=53	=113

CONCLUSION

Family, sex, social class, and religion have some impact upon the political attitudes of the Puerto Rican university student. Of these four variables, social class shows the least relationship to political attitudes and behavior. As was expected, male students are more likely than their female counterparts to be both leftist and politically active. The data indicate that there is a considerable degree of political inheritance among the students. There is also some indication that students who are, in a sense, breaking their family ties are also tending in political directions opposite to those of their fathers.

As measured by the almost total absence of support for the Christian Action party, the Roman Catholic Church in Puerto Rico has failed to impress its will upon the politics of both the general populace and the students. Nonetheless, religiosity, as shown by the data, does have a distinct effect upon political attitudes. In general, it can be said that the less religious the student, the more likely he is to consider himself leftist and to support the PIP. This relationship holds true regardless of the educational background of the parents or the sex of the student. Conversely, religiosity seems to be associated with a rightist position.

Given these findings, it becomes important to seek other variables that may provide a clearer picture of the determinants of student political behavior. It is time to examine the university experience itself and its effects upon the students.

Chapter IV

THE UNIVERSITY EXPERIENCE

The university, like schools on lower levels, may be regarded as a socializing agency for the adolescents continually entering and exiting. It takes many persons of the same age with similar status desires, provides them with a relatively homogeneous environment, and at the same time isolates them to varying degrees from the general community. The university exercises control over the students because of its power over the access to the highly desired goal, the degree. It would seem likely that the university has a major impact upon the values, attitudes, and opinions of its students.

It is evident from the popular literature, as well as from other sources, that all universities are not equally effective in shaping a desired end product and do not all have the same end product as a goal.[1] Further, not only may the products of two different universities differ, but the products of the same university may also differ, depending upon such factors as curriculum, living arrangements, and grades. We should therefore examine those factors on the campus of the University of Puerto Rico that may bear upon the politics of the students there.

Knowledge of the university itself is essential to an understand-

[1] See Nevitt Sanford, ed., *The American College*. The most extensive American survey to date of the literature on the impacts of colleges upon their students is Theodore M. Newcombe and K. A. Feldman, "The Impacts of Colleges upon Their Students," a report to the Carnegie Foundation for the Advancement of Teaching, January, 1968.

ing of how it influences its students. The University of Puerto Rico is an urban university located in the Río Piedras section of San Juan, the capital and largest city of Puerto Rico. While attending the university, the overwhelming majority of the students must live in or near San Juan, because the dormitory facilities of the university are limited to 370 students. Many of the students who do not live with their families or relatives rent rooms or apartments in the Río Piedras section. As a result, there are very few places where large numbers of the 18,000 students can regularly congregate. The recent erection of a student center has helped to alleviate this situation, but does not change the fact that the student is primarily an urban resident commuting to the university.

The architecture and sprawling nature of the campus reflect the rapid growth of the university, particularly since World War II. Situated in the center of the campus between the older section and the newer additions, next to the library, is a slum replete with tin shacks, chickens, seminaked children, and hanging laundry. The residents moved into this area before the university decided to expand. When it did expand, the authorities were reluctant to evict these squatters. Therefore, as the students move among their air-conditioned modern buildings and well-kept Spanish-style structures, the slum in their midst is a constant reminder of the plight of many of their countrymen. Leftist students have occasionally held rallies in this slum, partly because of the political backdrop that it provides.

It is difficult to imagine that this bustling, sprawling campus, with a student body over 18,000, began its life in 1902 with only 154 students studying to become teachers. The future teachers, however, provide the link between past and present. The School of Education has the largest enrollment (3,130), and these students seem to set the tone of the campus regarding attitudes, as well as style of dress—starched shirts, ties and jackets, stiff crinolines, and high heels are predominant on the campus. The students of the second largest school, Business (2,679), resemble the education students in dress, bearing, and the preprofessional aura that surrounds them. The very few quasi-beatniks that do exist seem mainly to be based in the Schools of Social Science (1,646) and Humanities (868).[2]

PREVAILING POLITICAL CLIMATE

The prevailing political milieu on the campus seems related to the political predispositions of the students at the end of their student "life cycles." Theodore Newcombe's study at Bennington College illustrates the success of a college community in changing the politicoeconomic attitudes of its inhabitants during their four-year tenure. The general tendency was for the coeds to become more liberal during the course of their college life. Movement toward liberalism meant for the Bennington student movement toward conformity with the dominant political view of the campus community.[3] Conducted more than two decades later, a study of students at the University of California at Berkeley shows that on that liberal campus the percentage of students identified as moderately or highly libertarian increased with additional years of schooling.[4] Another study of students from eleven universities documents the influence of the campus atmosphere during the 1950's upon the politics of the students. Students whose party preferences differed from their fathers were most likely to adopt the party preferences that were dominant on their respective campuses.[5] A panel study of Cornell students from 1950 to 1952 illustrates the pressures toward conservatism on a predominantly conservative campus. During that time, the student who was initially conservative remained so, however weak his original commitment. The staunch liberal also retained his position, but the apathetic liberal and the straddler were likely to have moved toward conservatism.[6] Evidence from a study of the National University of Colombia points to the politicizing and radicalizing in-

[2] Interviews with students and faculty and personal observation.

[3] Theodore M. Newcombe, *Personality and Social Change*, p. 147.

[4] Hannan Selvin and Warren O. Hagstrom, "Determinants of Support for Civil Liberties," *British Journal of Sociology*, 11 (March, 1960), p. 58.

[5] R. K. Goldsen *et al.*, *What College Students Think*, pp. 102–103.

[6] *Ibid.*, pp. 117–119.

fluence of a campus upon Latin American students. At this campus leftism, as measured by support for Castro, grew with the length of time the student attended the university. This tendency was even more striking for those who did not reside at home.[7]

Political Atmosphere of the University of Puerto Rico

As indicated earlier, the prevailing atmosphere at the University of Puerto Rico is one of center-conservatism. It can be recalled that on three indicators of student political attitudes—party preference, relative political position, and the student referendum—the left was far from being dominant among the students. In fact, almost a majority preferred the middle position, and the right had more support than the left.

Not only is the student body conservative in nature, but political activity is discouraged on the Río Piedras campus. In order to understand this state of affairs, it is necessary to realize that the University of Puerto Rico is dissimilar to public universities in Latin America. Partisan political activities and organizations are banned from the campus.[8] The students, until recently, were prohibited from having a university-wide student government and have virtually no voice in the running of the university. During the near quarter-century in which he has been chancellor, Jaime Benítez has defined the university as a "house of studies." A "house of studies," according to him, is one in which political activity is discouraged so that the major functions of the university, learning and studying, may be performed without any interference.[9]

In many ways, Benítez' policy of "house of studies" is a reaction to the situation that prevailed at the University of Puerto Rico before the PPD came to power in 1940. During the 1930's politics was a prominent feature of campus life. Faculty and administrators

[7] Kenneth N. Walker, "Determinants of Castro Support among Latin American University Students," *Social and Economic Studies*, 14, no. 1 (March, 1965), pp. 99–100.

[8] University of Puerto Rico, *Ley universitaria y reglamentos*, 1962, chapter 10.

[9] Jaime Benítez, *La casa de estudios*, p. 5.

received their appointments on the basis of party loyalty. Students were actively involved in politics. Political pressure was used to obtain high grades and easy examinations. Some students made careers out of student politics, remaining at the university for years and taking only one or two courses now and then. Classroom attendance was not obligatory, which further facilitated political activity among the students. In this era the followers of Albizu Campos' Nationalist party appeared to be the dominant element among the students. Many students, including Jaime Benítez, the current chancellor of the University of Puerto Rico, went to class wearing the black shirts of the Nationalist party. Rexford Tugwell, who was governor of Puerto Rico and briefly chancellor of the university, described what transpired at the university as "a parody of the educational process."[10]

Jaime Benítez, a close associate of Muñoz Marín and a leading member of the PPD, was appointed chancellor in 1942. He dedicated himself to the improvement of the university and to making the university more accessible to students from the lower-middle and working classes. During his tenure the number of full-time students more than tripled.

It was not until after World War II that a major showdown between Chancellor Benítez and the student political activists— mainly proindependence students—occurred. In 1946, six thousand students (or about two-thirds of the student body at the Río Piedras campus) held a one-day strike to protest President Truman's veto of a bill passed by the island's legislature that designated Spanish as the official language of instruction in the schools of Puerto Rico.[11]

The disturbance that has most affected the current student generation occurred about one year later. On December 17, 1947, a demonstration was held at the University of Puerto Rico to mark the return of Pedro Albizu Campos, who had just completed a six-year prison term for conspiracy to overthrow United States rule in Puerto Rico by force and violence. During the course of this demonstration, the American flag on the university tower was lowered,

10 Rexford G. Tugwell, *The Stricken Land*, pp. 108–110.
11 *New York Times*, November 9, 1946.

and in its place the Nationalists' one-star banner was raised. Three of the student leaders, including the president of the student body, were suspended indefinitely. The campus was restive but did not explode until a few months later, when Benítez denied permission for Albizu Campos, his former political idol, to speak on the campus. Benítez accused the Communists and the Nationalists of using fascist tactics to foment the disturbances. A student strike was declared and the classrooms were invaded. Clashes occurred between students and police, and the university was officially closed. Faculty and administration officials who were interviewed estimated that three to five thousand students were actively involved.

An immediate consequence of this strike was the expulsion or suspension of many of the politically active students. Many others lost credits for a year of college work. Such sanctions as these are not taken lightly in a society that so highly evaluates a college degree. Chancellor Benítez also took measures to prevent future disturbances. The university-wide student government was dissolved. The student newspaper was shut down. All partisan political activities were banned from the campus, and outside political speakers were denied admission to the campus. Student organizations and meetings were allowed on campus only if they engaged in no partisan propaganda and demonstrated a sincere attitude toward what Benítez called "good politics." Also, class attendance was made obligatory.[12]

A major consequence of these sanctions and restrictions was a decrease in student political activity. The hardest hit were the Nationalists and the proindependence students. The climate created

[12] Gordon K. Lewis, *Puerto Rico: Freedom and Power in the Caribbean*, pp. 454–455; *New York Times*, December 18, 1947, April 16, 1948, May 9, 1948; interviews with Puerto Ricans who were students at the time. University regulations require student organizations to furnish membership lists annually and to request annually for recognition as a campus organization. Furthermore, to discourage political activity among students and part-time students, the regulations place limitations on office holders in student organizations. Anyone who wishes to hold an office in a university-recognized campus organization must (a) have no less than a *C* average, (b) carry no less than twelve credits, and (c) be a student in good standing a year prior to his election (University of Puerto Rico, *Ley universitaria y reglamentos*, 1962, p. 78.).

by the loss of student leaders and the banning of organizations was not conducive to political activism and radicalism among the students. Only recently have the activities of FUPI (University Federation for Independence, a militant student group) and the growth of a movement for university reform helped to encourage renewed political discussion and activity on the campus. However, the number of students or faculty actively involved in politics is still small.

THE INTELLECTUAL CLIMATE

The intellectual climate at a university also influences the political behavior of its students. Professor Lipset discusses the relevance of academic standards to student politics: "The greater the pressure placed on students to work hard to retain their position in the university . . . the less they will participate in politics of any kind. . . . Students are also more available for politics in universities which do not hold the undergraduates to a demanding syllabus."[13] The situation at the University of Puerto Rico seems at variance with Professor Lipset's hypothesis. The university is not intellectually demanding for most students, yet they tend to shy away from political activity and radical politics.

Observers both inside and outside the university have been critical of the intellectual standards prevailing at the University of Puerto Rico.[14] The textbook-lecture method is in widespread use. Students who carry programs running from eighteen to twenty-four hours a week rarely read a book other than their text.[15] The number of books checked out of the library by each student averages about two per year.[16] There is little class discussion, and students routinely accept what they have heard in class. Grades are

[13] Seymour M. Lipset, "University Students and Politics in Underdeveloped Countries," *Minerva*, 3, no. 1 (Autumn, 1964), 38.

[14] The following is derived primarily from Luis Nieves Falcón, *Recruitment to Higher Education in Puerto Rico, 1940–1960*, chapters 2, 3, 5, 6, and 7; Lewis, *Freedom and Power*, pp. 151–462; and interviews with students and faculty.

[15] Frank Bowles, "The High Cost of Low-Cost Education," in *Higher Education in the United States*, ed. S. E. Harris, pp. 199–200.

[16] Falcón, *Recruitment to Higher Education*, p. 134.

thought of as ends in themselves. Many students take heavy course loads only to drop some prior to the final examination. This can be done without penalty and is a safeguard to the student's grade point average.[17] Some professors who were interviewed commented on the widespread cheating and plagiarism of papers.

Student informants report that conversations in the cafeteria and the student center rarely touch upon academic, intellectual, or political concerns. Avante-garde foreign movies shown on campus are sparsely attended, but a film like *Carousel* is sold out. The university bookstore lacks a good paperback collection or, for that matter, a good hardback collection of books other than required or recommended texts in the humanities, social sciences, and natural sciences. There are few bookshops, new or secondhand, in the immediate vicinity of the campus. In interviews students, faculty, and administrative personnel often criticized the nonintellectual student body.

The university has found that the ever growing number of students brings its problems. More and more of the entering students are found deficient in one or more subjects. Valuable time and effort must be spent on remedial courses to bring students already enrolled to entrance level. In part, this is a function of the admissions requirements of the University of Puerto Rico. Candidates for admission must have at least an overall *C* average and must take an examination administered by the College Entrance Examination Board. A candidate need not have taken a college preparatory curriculum in secondary school in order to gain admission.[18] In various schools, special honors programs have been instituted for those students desirous of going to a professional or graduate school on the mainland. Their chances of their being admitted and surviving in such institutions would be low if they relied on the university's normal curriculum.

The findings of a study done in the late 1950's at the University of Puerto Rico on the intellectual motivations and attitudes among

[17] Bowles, "High Cost of Low-Cost Education," pp. 200–201.
[18] University of Puerto Rico, *Bulletin of General Information, 1964–1965,* p. 44.

the students support the conclusions reached on the basis of this researcher's observations and interviews. The earlier study found that "there was general agreement that students lack motivation, have little intellectual enthusiasm, and tend to be apathetic toward scholarship."[19]

The faculty and administration have also come under criticism because of the state of affairs at the university. Only about 20 percent of the faculty have Ph.D.'s; about 30 percent have B.A.'s and the remainder M.A.'s They have heavy teaching loads, take on extra-university work, and engage in very little research. Many of the faculty are themselves graduates of the University of Puerto Rico and consequently lack different perspectives. Also, a large proportion of the faculty are women who divide their energies between their professorial and household duties. Faculty members have found that the ladder to success is not through publication or brilliant teaching, but through personal relationships that may lead to administrative appointments. Such a faculty makes little demand upon the time or the intellect of the students.

The intellectual climate is further clouded by ever present bickering, backbiting, and infighting. The faculty is divided in its loyalty to Chancellor Benítez. Many feel that he runs the University of Puerto Rico as his private property. Criticism has been leveled against him for his alleged failure to consult the faculty on matters concerning faculty appointments, salaries, and university policies. He nominates and supervises both the teaching and administrative staffs at all three campuses of the University of Puerto Rico.[20] The Faculty Senate is accused of being a rubber stamp for

[19] William H. Knowles, "Manpower and Education in Puerto Rico," in *Manpower and Education*, ed. Frederick Harbison and Charles A. Myers, p. 125.

[20] On January 20, 1966, Governor Roberto Sánchez Vilella signed a law reorganizing the government of the university. Under this law, the university was divided into three autonomous campuses, each with its own chancellor. The university itself was to be headed by a university president who nominates the chancellors. Each campus was also to have its own Academic Senate, which must be consulted prior to the nomination of the chancellor. After two other candidates had declined, Chancellor Benítez was elected president by a five-to-four vote of the Council of Higher Education. Also included in this reform bill

Chancellor Benítez. Its lack of independence was evident for many when it voted against the faculty consulted in the appointment of a chancellor.[21] The administration claims that the faculty critics are a vocal and politically ambitious minority of the faculty of one campus (Río Piedras). One dean pointed out that this faculty had two-thirds of the votes in the Faculty Senate and that there was nothing to stop them from voting any way they chose. Most of the opposition to Benítez is drawn from the faculties of the Schools of Humanities and Social Sciences. They have boycotted the Faculty Senate in protest against the chancellor's policies and the weakness of the senate. Members of these faculties have also been at the forefront of a drive for university reform. The meaning of university reform for most of the faculty and students committed to it is the clipping of Chancellor Benítez' power.

In general, the climate on the Río Piedras campus is unconducive to the search for knowledge or to the stimulation of student minds. Student as well as faculty morale is low. In this nonstimulating and undemanding environment, students do not turn their attention to politics or political activity, but to obtaining a degree as quickly and as painlessly as possible.[22]

The University of Puerto Rico may appear typical of large, rapidly growing state universities. However, the University of Puerto Rico is not one of several hundred alternatives like a state university on the mainland; it is the major source of higher education on the island. The vast majority of teachers, government officials, engineers, and professionals has graduated from the University of Puerto Rico. It is the most prestigious institution of higher education on the island. Yet, for the most part, its students seem

---

was a measure requiring the election of campus-wide student councils on each of the three campuses (*New York Times*, March 6, 1966).

21 José Arsenio Torres, "UPR: Will It Get Worse?" *San Juan Review*, 2, no. 5 (June, 1965), 22–24, 68.

22 One of my interviewees was a dedicated member of FUPI who had just graduated. Although he had been politically active during his last year or two of college, he had curtailed his political activity because of his desire to graduate as soon as possible. He graduated in three years.

oblivious to their own intellectual development. It is from this pool that the island's business, political, and cultural elite are drawn.

The situation in Puerto Rico is mirrored in the Philippines. The Philippines was acquired by the United States at the same time as Puerto Rico, and its educational system, like Puerto Rico's, was shaped by Americans. It too is dedicated to expansion of higher education; the Philippines has one of the world's highest enrollments in terms of the proportion of college-age youths attending college. Philippine students have been criticized in a similar manner to Puerto Rican students. "Criticism by visitors to Philippine classrooms has been directed at the students' undue dependence on the teacher's word, and to a lesser degree upon the text, their aim being to absorb and repeat the same words in examinations and recitations."[23] The final parallel is that Philippine students, like their Puerto Rican counterparts, have been noted for their political docility.[24]

THE SUBSYSTEMS OF THE UNIVERSITY

When a student attends a large university, the impact of the university as a whole is often subordinate to that of the particular subsystem of which the student is a member. It is therefore pertinent to examine these subsystems and the possible political effects of membership in them. It is such subsystems as fraternities and sororities that do the major job of socialization. Studies conducted at Berkeley and nine other universities with fraternities and sororities revealed that members were more likely to be conservative than were independents on each campus. Also, fraternity members became progressively less liberal during the course of their student careers.[25] Fraternities, it would seem, select the more conservative as members and socialize their members toward conservative

[23] Arthur Carson, *Higher Education in the Philippines*, U.S. Department of Health, Education, and Welfare, Office of Education, Bulletin 1961, no. 29, p. 172.

[24] *Ibid.*; Carl H. Lande, "The Philippines," in *Education and Political Development*, ed. J. S. Coleman, pp. 316–317.

[25] Selvin and Hagstrom, "Support for Civil Liberties," p. 69; Goldsen *et al.*, *What College Students Think*, p. 123.

norms and values. Former Senator Barry Goldwater, among others, has remarked upon the relationship between fraternities and conservatism on campuses.

There are about twenty fraternities at the University of Puerto Rico. According to student, faculty, and administration interviewees, they tend to have a conservative orientation. The fraternities campaigned in the referendum for the alternative placing restrictions on student political activities. Recently, there was a minor scandal when leading fraternities were found to have discriminated against darker-skinned Puerto Ricans. Members of fraternities who were interviewed tended to support either the PPD or the PER, and none considered himself a leftist.

However, fraternities are not very important at the University of Puerto Rico and membership in them is relatively small. One subsystem that does involve every student and does seem to be important is the faculty or college that the student attends. At the University of Puerto Rico, every full-time four-year student spends his freshman year in the Faculty of General Studies, where he is exposed to a variety of liberal arts courses. The remainder of his undergraduate career is spent primarily at one college, the College of Education or the Faculty of Social Sciences, for example. From sophomore to senior year, most courses are taken at the school and most of the student's classmates are also enrolled in that school. It is reasonable to expect that the school that the student attends for three-fourths of his college life is likely to have a major impact upon his politics and his views of the world.

Table 39 shows the relationship between the schools and the political positions of the students vis-à-vis each other. One striking item indicated by this table is the division of the faculties into two camps: those faculties with a large proportion of students who consider themselves leftist and those faculties with a comparatively small proportion considering themselves leftist. Students in the Schools of Humanities, Law, and Social Science are more likely than students in the other schools to feel that they are to the left politically. These students are also less likely than those in other schools to take a center position. However, students in the Schools

TABLE 39
School and Relative Political Position

School	N		Relative Political Position			Total
			Left	Center	Right	
Social Science	65	%	43	34	23	100
Law	96	%	40	27	32	99*
Humanities	44	%	27	43	30	100
Medicine	12	%	17	50	33	100
Education	83	%	13	53	34	100
Engineering	66	%	12	52	36	100
Natural Science	50	%	12	62	26	100
Business	62	%	10	55	36	101*
General Studies	50	%	8	56	36	100

of Engineering, General Studies, and Business are more likely to consider themselves rightists. Generally, though, there is little difference among the various schools with regard to the percentage of students identifying themselves as right. It should also be noted that in all the schools but social science and law the modal position is the center. This may reflect the apolitical nature of the students in these schools as well as the politicization of the students in social science and law.

The 1965 elections for the student presidents of the Schools of Social Science and Business provided further evidence of the political split between schools. A member of the militantly leftist FUPI won at the School of Social Science; a Cuban exile and member of the rightist FAU (University Federation of Anti-Communists) was elected president of the School of Business.

When party preference was related to the respondents' school, the data reveal a similar division among the students (see Table 40). Again, students in the Schools of Humanities, Law, and Social Science are more likely to support the PIP, than students in the Schools of Business, Engineering, General Studies, and Natural Sciences, who are more likely to favor parties on the right of the political spectrum.

How do these results compare with those found among students elsewhere? A study of students at the National University of

Colombia reveals that students in the Faculties of Law and Economics tend to be more leftist than their peers in other faculties, whereas those in the natural sciences tend to be least leftist.[26] A study of four schools at the University of Chile in Santiago indicates that proportionately more leftists are in the School of History and that relatively the fewest are in the School of Engineering. In none of the four schools at the University of Chile does the proportion of rightist students reach more than 6 percent.[27] In Venezuela, engineering students are reported to be the most conservative.[28] At the National University in Mexico, the Economics Faculty, which includes sociology, is further left than any other faculty, followed by law. Students in commerce, engineering, and medicine tend to be conservative in their responses. The most radical faculty at the University of Buenos Aires is the Faculty of Letters and Philosophy, which includes many sociology students.[29]

In the United States, many studies indicate that students in the social sciences and humanities are more liberal than those in business, engineering, and the natural sciences.[30] In the 1965 student

TABLE 40
School and Party Preference

School	N		PIP	PPD	PER	PAC	Total
Social Science	66	%	52	24	23	2	101*
Humanities	42	%	38	52	10	—	100
Law	92	%	38	36	25	1	100
Engineering	69	%	16	54	30	—	100
Education	88	%	16	64	16	5	101*
Business	70	%	14	46	40	—	100
Natural Science	48	%	13	52	31	5	101*
General Studies	52	%	12	52	31	6	101*
Medicine	13	%	—	62	31	8	101*

[26] Robert C. Williamson, *El estudiante colombiano y sus actitudes*, p. 75.

[27] Myron Glazer, "The Professional and Political Attitudes of Chilean University Students," Ph.D. dissertation, Princeton University, 1965, p. 216.

[28] Walter S. Washington, "Student Politics in Latin America: The Venezuelan Example," *Foreign Affairs*, 37 (1959), 464.

[29] Lipset, "University Students and Politics," pp. 34–35.

[30] Newcombe and Feldman, *Impacts of Colleges*, pp. 162–164, 459–464.

demonstrations at the University of California, social science and humanities students were most likely to support the Free Speech Movement, whereas support for a conservative position was most likely to be found among students in business administration, engineering, architecture, and agriculture.[31] There is no total agreement, however, regarding the hypothesis that social science and humanities students are more liberal than students in other fields. Philip E. Jacob, in a general survey of American college students, claims that "for the most part, the values and outlook of students do not vary greatly whether they have pursued a conventional liberal arts program, an integrated general education curriculum or one of the strictly professional-vocational options."[32] The findings regarding the relationship between field of study and politics for Puerto Rican students thus somewhat resemble those from studies of students in Latin America and the United States, despite some inconsistencies and sketchiness in these studies.

There are two possible explanations for the relationship between field of studies and political leaning. It could be hypothesized that students with a left-wing orientation are more attracted initially to certain fields of study, while those with right-wing orientation are more attracted to other fields. On the other hand, it seems equally plausible that certain fields socialize their inductees toward a particular political position. The ideal manner in which to explore these contrasting hypotheses—selection versus socialization—would have been through a panel study. Since it was not possible, given this research design, the best alternative was to employ the increasing length of time in a particular curriculum as indicative of increasing exposure to the orientation of that school. The students were divided according to whether they were pursuing a liberal arts or a non–liberal arts curriculum, as well as by the number of years they have been enrolled at the university.

Table 41 shows that at each time period the liberal arts students

[31] Robert H. Sommers, "The Mainsprings of the Rebellion: A Survey of Berkeley Students in November 1964," in *The Berkeley Student Revolt: Facts and Interpretations,* ed. Seymour M. Lipset, and Sheldon S. Wolin, p. 545.

[32] Philip E. Jacob, *Changing Values in College,* p. 3.

TABLE 41

Influence of Years in University and School† on Student's Political Position

| | Years in University | | | |
| | | -3 | | 3+ |
Student's Political Position	Liberal Arts %	Non–Liberal Arts %	Liberal Arts %	Non–Liberal Arts %
Left	30	13	42	11
Center	46	56	27	52
Right	24	31	31	37
Total	100	100	100	100
	=67	=162	=139	=109

† Liberal arts include the Schools of Humanities, Social Science, and Law; non–liberal arts include the Schools of Business, Education, Natural Science, Medicine, and Engineering. The School of General Studies has been omitted since all students in it are freshmen who have not yet entered their major school.

are more likely than the non–liberal arts students to be leftist. Conversely, more non–liberal arts than liberal arts students are rightist at each time period. Length of time in school seems to have a differential impact. For those enrolled in the non–liberal arts schools, the length of time at the university appears to have little effect on their political identification. Those in school three years or less are very similar to those who have attended longer, although over a time there is a slight decline in the percentage identifying themselves as leftist and a 6 percent increase in students considering themselves to the right. Time has more of an impact upon the liberal arts students. Students "older" in terms of time at the university, compared with the "younger" students, are more likely to be leftist. Contrary to expectations, the "older" ones are also slightly more likely to be rightist. The liberal arts students become more polarized with the passage of time. In general, the data indicate that pursuit of a liberal arts rather than a non–liberal arts curriculum seems to orient the student toward politics left of center.

When political party preference is considered, the data as seen

TABLE 42
Influence of Years in University and School on Student's Party Preference

	Years in University			
	−3		3+	
Student's	Liberal Arts	Non–Liberal Arts	Liberal Arts	Non–Liberal Arts
Party Preference	%	%	%	%
PIP	44	15	42	14
PPD	33	49	36	62
PER	21	33	21	23
PAC	2	3	1	1
Total	100	100	100	100
	=66	=170	=135	=115

in Table 42 reveal some patterns that differ from the previous table. As in Table 41, liberal arts students, compared with non–liberal arts students, regardless of the number of years in the university, are more likely to support the leftist PIP and less likely to prefer the centrist PPD. However, although non–liberal arts students, compared with liberal arts students, preferred the conservative PER, the difference between these two groupings among the "older" students was minimal. Contrary to the findings on relative political position, there were also few differences between the "older" and "younger" liberal arts students. However, among non–liberal arts students, there were noticeable differences between the "older" and "younger" students; the former were less likely than the latter to support the conservative PER and PAC and more likely to prefer the PPD, the center party.

In order to determine further the effect of a chosen field of study upon the political attitudes of the students, the respondents were asked whether they approved of student leaders representing the interests and ideologies of national political parties in student politics. In Table 43, as in the previous data, the liberal arts students as a whole, regardless of length of time at the university, took a more leftist position than their non–liberal arts peers. They were more likely to be in favor of student leaders representing the interest and ideologies of national political parties in student politics.

"Younger" students in both categories were more in favor of the leftist alternative than "older" students.

The students were also asked to indicate the change they desired most in their particular school. As seen in Table 44, liberal arts students at both time periods are more likely than non–liberal arts students to name greater academic freedom and increased student participation in university government. On the other hand, non–liberal arts students, more than liberal arts students, name such

TABLE 43

Attitude toward Student Leaders and National Parties by School and by Year

Responses to: "Is it all right for student leaders to represent the interests
and ideologies of national political
parties in student politics?"

	Years in School			
	−3		3+	
	Liberal Arts %	Non–Liberal Arts %	Liberal Arts %	Non–Liberal Arts %
Yes	44	28	36	23
No	56	72	64	77
Total	100 =69	100 =171	100 =140	100 =177

TABLE 44

Desired School Changes by School and Year

	Years in School			
	−3		3+	
Desired Changes	Liberal Arts %	Non–Liberal Arts %	Liberal Arts %	Non–Liberal Arts %
Recreational facilities	5	8	1	9
Educational facilities	12	25	21	27
Educational training	29	42	45	35
Academic freedom and participation	54	25	33	29
Total	100 =56	100 =139	100 =126	100 =107

practical changes as improvement in recreational and educational facilities. There are only slight differences between the "younger" and "older" non–liberal arts students in terms of changes desired. However, sharp differences between the "younger" and "older" liberal arts students are apparent. "Older" liberal arts students are less desirous of greater academic freedom and increased student participation in university government than their "younger" counterparts. In terms of desired school changes, the "older" liberal arts student begins to resemble both "older" and "younger" non–liberal arts students.

Although the effect of length of time in a curriculum has not been consistent, the data are clear on one point. The liberal arts student, however long he has been enrolled, is more politically involved at both national and university levels than the non–liberal arts student. With respect to national politics, the liberal arts student is likely to discuss national politics more often than the non–liberal arts student and much more likely to be a member of a national political party. In most of these instances the "older" students (particularly liberal arts students) tend to be more politically involved than the "younger" ones. When national political involvement was measured on the basis of responses to a scale made up of items dealing with the respondent's interest and involvement in national political affairs, the data indicated that the liberal arts students were again more likely than their non–liberal arts peers to be highly involved in national politics and that this was true for each year while at the university.

At the university level, the liberal arts student is more likely than his non–liberal arts counterpart to be interested in student politics, to have voted in his school election, and to have attended a meeting of his student council. When a scale was used that employed items dealing with participation in student politics (including demonstrations), as well as items dealing with the frequency of discussion and interest in student politics, the percentage of liberal arts students involved was considerably higher[33] than the

[33] "Higher" for this scale and the subsequent scale was determined by obtaining the mean score for all the students based upon the scores of all the or-

TABLE 45
Interest in Student Politics and Relative Political Position

| | Interest in Student Politics | | | |
| | Much | Some | Little | None |
Political Position	%	%	%	%
Left	51	19	10	11
Center	27	52	51	47
Right	22	29	39	42
Total	100	100	100	100
	=111	=205	=108	=53

percentage of non–liberal arts students. In every year after the first in college, about three-quarters of the liberal arts students were highly involved in student politics, whereas the percentage of highly involved non–liberal arts students ranged from 24 percent in the first year to 48 percent in the fourth to seventh years.

It is interesting to examine the manner in which interest in student politics is related to a student's political position. Table 45 shows that those who express the most interest in student politics are most likely to be leftist. Conversely, the less a student is interested in student politics the more likely he is to be rightist. Fifty-one percent of those most interested in student politics considered themselves leftist. Furthermore, uninterested students within each school were most likely to be rightist.

It has been shown that the liberal arts student is more likely to be left and less likely to be right or center than his non–liberal arts peer. Unfortunately, the data have not been consistent enough to determine whether selection or socialization contributed to these differences. However, the data do indicate that the non–liberal arts student becomes less leftist the longer he is in school. The differences between "younger" and "older" liberal arts students vary, depending upon the political item being examined. For example, on one traditional Latin American measure of student leftism—*co-*

---

dinal items composing the scale. Those students whose score was higher than the mean were considered to be highly involved.

gobierno (a demand for student parity in the governing of a university)—"younger" rather than "older" liberal arts students were, unexpectedly, more in favor of student participation in university government. It seems, in general, that selection of schools by students and socialization of the students by particular schools both govern where students will be on the political spectrum.

Whichever is the greater factor, selection or socialization, the political difference between liberal arts and non–liberal arts students still demands further explanation. Differences among the various faculties were therefore examined in order to determine whether these differences accounted for leftism among liberal arts students and conservatism among non–liberal arts students or for the initial selection of these schools by students of differing political persuasions.

Various hypotheses have been put forward to account for the political differences among faculties. Prominent among these is the economic argument, which states that students in fields offering them few opportunities to practice skills or make much money are more likely to be leftist and politically active than students in other fields.[34] In order to test this hypothesis, Puerto Rican students were divided by faculty and by the probability, as they saw it, of working in the occupation of their choice after graduation. As seen in Table 46, the number of expected opportunities bears little relationship to being leftist in terms of either self-identification or support for the PIP. Within each category of school, the percentage of leftist students is similar, regardless of whether they think there are many or just some opportunities available. Thus, contrary to findings among students elsewhere, in Japan and India, for example,[35] the political behavior of Puerto Rican students does not seem

34 Lipset, "University Students and Politics," p. 34; Edward Shils, "The Intellectuals in the Political Development of the New States," in *Political Change in Underdeveloped Countries: Nationalism and Communism*, ed. John H. Kautsky, pp. 201–205; Myron Weiner, *The Politics of Scarcity: Public Pressure and Political Response in India*, p. 184.

35 Shils, "Intellectuals in Political Development," p. 201–225; Michiya Shimbori, "Zengakureu: A Japanese Case Study of a Student Political Movement,"

TABLE 46
Influence of School and Opportunities in Field on Student's Politics

	Opportunities in Field			
	Many		Some	
	Liberal	Non–Liberal	Liberal	Non–Liberal
Student's Political	Arts	Arts	Arts	Arts
Position	%	%	%	%
Left	36	12	40	11
Center	34	52	34	66
Right	30	36	26	23
Total	100	100	100	100
	=135	=205	=65	=64
Student's Party				
Preference	%	%	%	%
PIP	40	15	45	11
PPD	37	54	32	58
PER	23	29	20	26
PAC	—	2	3	5
Total	100	100	100	100
	=131	=217	=65	=65

to vary according to the perceived range of opportunities to work in the occupation of their choice after graduation. This lack of variation may possibly be a function of the richness of career opportunities for Puerto Rican university graduates both in Puerto Rico and in the mainland United States. Therefore, even if a student responds in terms of "some" or "few" opportunities, he may still think it likely that he will get a remunerative position.[36]

Another possible reason for the differences between the faculties is the nature of the training. Professor Lipset asserts that "students engaged in the courses of study which entail some apprenticeship

---

Sociology of Education, 37, no. 2 (Spring, 1964), 323–325; Weiner, *Politics of Scarcity*, p. 184.

[36] Knowles cites the expansion in the industrial groups utilizing highly educated personnel that has occurred from 1950 to 1960. He also asserts that many Puerto Rican college graduates go to the mainland after graduation to gain experience and that later many of these return (Knowles, "Manpower and Education," pp. 110, 113–115).

for a definite profession, e.g. engineering, medicine and preparation for secondary school teaching . . . are less likely to be rebellious than students in courses without determinate destinations."[37] This hypothesis receives some support in the case of the Puerto Rican students. In all of the non–liberal arts schools, the training is directed toward a definite occupation that the student will be able to practice as soon as he graduates. This is true for the Schools of Business, Education, Engineering, Medicine, and Natural Sciences. The situation is somewhat different as far as the liberal arts faculties are concerned, except for the Law School. In both the social sciences and the humanities, students must go further in their educations in order to practice as professionals. The nature of the training does not lead most students to consider themselves apprentices in their field. That is, sociology students, for example, could not perform as sociologists in any meaningful way upon graduation. Also, the nature of their training does not direct them toward a definite profession, as would be true in the case of students in the School of Education or even the School of Natural Sciences. It would therefore seem that those students who are already involved in training for their chosen profession and for whom satisfactory socialization has already begun would be most likely to have made commitments to their future careers and to the societal status quo.

The difference in academic standards among faculties also contributes to differential political behavior among students; theoretically, the less demanding the student's curriculum, the more time he has for political activity. As mentioned earlier, the University of Puerto Rico has come under criticism for its low academic standards. This does not mean, however, that the criticism applies equally to all schools. The Schools of Medicine, Natural Sciences, Engineering, and Law are considered to have higher academic standards than any other schools at the University of Puerto Rico. Education, business, and, to some extent, social sciences have acquired reputations as being easy for students. Dividing these schools ac-

[37] Lipset, "University Students and Politics," p. 34.

cording to reputed academic standards and then correlating them with the proportion of leftist students brings mixed results. The School of Education has a relatively small proportion of students who are leftist, yet it is regarded as the school with the lowest academic standards. On the other hand, three of the four schools noted for their relatively high academic standards have comparatively few leftists among their student bodies.

One factor that does seem to differentiate the schools with a relatively large proportion of leftists from those with comparatively few is the nature of the subject matter.[38] In the Schools of Social Science, Humanities, and Law, students study subjects dealing with man, his values, his social relationships, and his society. The students in these schools are also more likely to confront the problems of Puerto Rico during the course of their studies. One urban student told of a shock that he had received while working on a sociology project in the previously unfamiliar rural area. During the course of the study, he noticed that the land law, which limits holdings to a maximum of five hundred acres per person, was being violated. In addition, he claimed that many acres on these large farms were lying fallow while neighboring peasants desired more land and food for themselves. Although not all students in these schools have such dramatic experiences, many during the course of their studies are exposed to social problems and inequities that students in such schools as natural sciences or engineering are never forced to confront. Students in business, engineering, and other non–liberal arts schools also have less opportunity to read Puerto Rican novelists and essayists in their course work. Liberal arts students are more likely than non–liberal arts students to read the works of such men as René Marqués, who bitterly indict the Puerto Rican system and write of the damage that colonialism has done to the Puerto Rican

---

[38] The strain between the orientation of the left and the subject matter of the non–liberal arts schools was reported by an active member of FUPI who had been enrolled in the School of Business for two years, primarily because of family pressures. For him, being both a radical activist and a business student placed him in such a conflict that he finally withdrew from school and joined the staff of a small leftist magazine.

people. A reading of Puerto Rican history may also cause the student to question the nature of the status quo. As one history student in the School of Humanities said, "How can one read the history of Puerto Rico and not favor independence for Puerto Rico?"

Liberal arts students view society from a perspective different from that of their non–liberal arts peers. As one professor in the School of Social Sciences expressed it: "Once a student takes an objective look, a social scientific perspective on his environment, he realizes that Puerto Rico is a colony. It may be a gilded colony but it is still a colony. Once confronted by this fact he must come to terms with it. He will either accept it and continue with his life and career like anyone else or he will support the idea of independence for Puerto Rico."[39]

The professors in the different schools may also contribute to the differences between liberal arts students and non–liberal arts students. Professors in the liberal arts schools tend to be more critical of the status quo of the university, as well as of the society, than their colleagues in the other schools. It should be recalled that, as stated earlier, the faculty of the Schools of Social Sciences and Humanities have boycotted the Faculty Senate in protest of Chancellor Benítez' policies. All the professors in the School of Social Sciences who were interviewed professed *independentista* leanings. Many were politically active. One was a PIP representative on the San Juan City Council, and several others were left-of-center PPD members of the island legislature. Conversely, none of the professors in the non–liberal arts schools who were interviewed expressed proindependence feelings. Many were supporters of statehood. Few expressed criticism of Chancellor Benítez and few were politically active. In such non–liberal arts schools as business, a large proportion of the faculty worked in industry at the same time as they

[39] A similar process seems to operate among Puerto Rican students who have gone to the United States. Several students who were interviewed in Puerto Rico and the United States claimed that they had become proindependence supporters while studying in the United States. One student left Puerto Rico an *estadista* and returned an *independentista*; he said that observing Puerto Rico from abroad gave him new perspectives and led him to become a supporter of independence and a leftist as far as Puerto Rican society was concerned.

taught at the university. These men considered themselves practical men of affairs and were highly critical of the activities of their proindependence colleagues in the liberal arts colleges.[40]

In summary, the University of Puerto Rico and the nature of its student body have not provided a context conducive to student activism. Rightist students outnumber leftists and both appear to be drawn from different bases within the university. The former are more likely to be students in the non–liberal arts schools, whereas the latter are more likely to come from the liberal arts schools. This may be attributed to the nature of the subject matter and the extent of preparation required for a future career, as well as to the politics of the teachers in the different schools. The absence of longitudinal data makes it difficult to differentiate between the effects of socialization in a field and selection of a field by a specific type of student.

SATISFACTION AS A STUDENT

The extent to which a student is satisfied with his life as a student is another factor that must be considered when dealing with those variables that influence his politics. Newspapers and popular magazines often give accounts of student demonstrations both in the United States and in Latin America that were sparked by unpopular regulations or difficult examinations. All universities are faced with the fact that the role of student is full of tensions and anxieties. Student discontent in itself, however, is no guarantee of increased political activity in general or support for the left in particular.

The findings from previous studies as to the relationship between student dissatisfaction and frustration on the one hand and politics

---

[40] The effect that a group of professors can have on college students can be seen in relationship between the History Department of Rutgers University and the Rutgers chapter of Students for a Democratic Society (SDS). This department (New Brunswick campus) vis-à-vis other departments of the university has a relatively higher proportion of articulate leftist professors; the SDS chapter at Rutgers derives a large proportion of its student membership, and especially its leadership, from the History Department.

on the other are not very clear or consistent. Students in Southeast Asia have not generally released their frustrations and tensions into the political arena.[41] University students in Mexico, Colombia, and Japan, on the other hand, do channel their frustrations into political activity.[42] At the University of California, during the Free Speech Movement of 1964, student leaders and other commentators focused upon dissatisfaction with the workings of the multiversity as a major source of student grievance. Yet, at the same time as this dissatisfaction was being cited, a survey of the Berkeley student body revealed a fairly satisfied campus. About four out of five student respondents (82%) claimed to be satisfied or very satisfied with their educational experience at Berkeley, including teachers, courses, and examinations. In addition, 92 percent agreed that "the president of this university and the chancellor are really trying very hard to provide top-quality educational experiences for the students here."[43] Yet during the course of the demonstrations large numbers of these relatively satisfied students participated.

Some analysts have felt that student unrest and political activity, particularly in the developing areas, might be a function of the lack of extracurricular activities. If these were present, the students' energy, frustrations, and need for self-assertion would be drained from politics.[44] However, when extracurricular activities were employed in American universities in the Near East and in Japan during the 1920's to help curb student political activities, these measures proved ineffective.[45] At Berkeley, the number of non-political activities available to the students was very large. At the University of Puerto Rico, the students can participate in many nonpolitical activities ranging from fraternities and intramural sports to choral and theatrical groups. In general, the presence or

[41] Joseph Fischer, "The University Student in South and Southeast Asia," *Minerva*, 2 (Autumn, 1963), p. 40.

[42] E. Wight Bakke, "Students on the March: The Cases of Mexico and Colombia," *Sociology of Education*, 37, no. 2 (Spring, 1964), 218–220; Shimbori, "Zengakureu: A Japanese Case Study," pp. 235–237.

[43] Sommers, "Mainsprings of the Rebellion," p. 536.

[44] Bakke, "Students on the March," p. 203.

[45] Lipset, "University Students and Politics," pp. 45–46.

absence of nonpolitical activities does not seem to be very significant to student political behavior. The whole issue of the overall relationship between the extent of student satisfaction and political activity obviously deserves more attention.

What about the situation at the University of Puerto Rico? When the entire sample is taken into account, the students tend to be satisfied with their life as students. Three out of four students claim to be satisfied or very satisfied with their professors, courses, and facilities. When asked whether they would enroll in their present field of specialization if they could begin their university studies over again, 82 percent of the students responded in the affirmative. Dissatisfaction with student life apparently affects only a minority at the University of Puerto Rico.

Despite the fact that the proportion of dissatisfied students at the University of Puerto Rico is relatively small, is there any relationship between the degree of satisfaction and political position and behavior? The data in Table 47 show that the dissatisfied student is more likely than the satisfied one to consider himself to the

TABLE 47
Satisfaction with Life as a Student and Student's Politics

Student's Political Position	Satisfaction of Student	
	Yes %	No %
Left	16	36
Center	51	32
Right	33	32
Total	100	100
	=395	=125
Student's Party Preference	%	%
PIP	20	36
PPD	49	45
PER	29	18
PAC	2	1
Total	100	100
	=407	=124

left of the student body. The satisfied student, however, is more likely than his dissatisfied peer to think of himself as being at the center. There is virtually no difference between satisfied and dissatisfied students in terms of the percentage considering themselves to the right. In terms of party preference, dissatisfied students were more likely than the satisfied ones to choose the leftist alternative, in this case the PIP. The proportion choosing the PIP among the dissatisfied students was almost two times as great as among the satisfied students. It is interesting to note that satisfaction-dissatisfaction does make a difference as far as preference for the PER, the conservative party, is concerned. Combining the percentages for the parties of the right, PER and PAC, the table shows that 31 percent of the satisfied students, compared with 19 percent of their dissatisfied colleagues, prefer these parties. There is only a slight difference between these two groups as far as preference for the PPD is concerned.

In order to ensure that these results were not primarily functions of the schools in which the students were enrolled, the respondents' schools were controlled for in Table 48. The data show that the liberal arts student is more likely than the non–liberal arts student to be dissatisfied—34 percent compared with 21 percent. Both groups of liberal arts students are more likely than either the satisfied or dissatisfied non–liberal arts students to consider themselves to the left of the general student body. However, within each group of schools, the dissatisfied student more than the satisfied student identifies himself as being on the left. As in Table 47, satisfaction or dissatisfaction makes little difference as far as self-identified right is concerned. Further, either group of liberal arts students is more likely than either group of non–liberal arts students to prefer the PIP. However, within each group of schools, the dissatisfied student is more likely than the satisfied one to prefer the PIP, particularly in the case of liberal arts students. Whether or not a student is satisfied seems to have little bearing on his preference for the PPD. Satisfaction or dissatisfaction with life as a student appears to have a differential effect on liberal arts and non–liberal

TABLE 48
Influence of School and Satisfaction as Student on Student's Politics

	Liberal Arts		Non–Liberal Arts	
	Satisfaction		Satisfaction	
Student's Political	Yes	No	Yes	No
Position	%	%	%	%
Left	29	54	9	23
Center	42	17	57	46
Right	29	29	34	31
Total	100	100	100	100
	=136	=69	=216	=56
Student's Party				
Preference	%	%	%	%
PIP	36	56	12	20
PPD	36	33	56	51
PER	27	11	29	27
PAC	2	—	3	2
Total	101*	100	100	100
	=135	=63	=230	=59

arts students as far as preference for conservative parties is concerned. Among the non–liberal arts students, the percentage choosing the PER and PAC is very similar for the satisfied and dissatisfied students. This is not true for the satisfied and dissatisfied liberal arts students; 29 percent of the satisfied ones prefer the PER and PAC, compared with 11 percent of the dissatisfied students.

The data in the above tables reveal that the dissatisfied student is more likely than his satisfied classmate to be leftist, regardless of whether the indicator is self-identification or party choice. When school is held constant, the data indicate that this trend is similar for students within each school grouping, although liberal arts students, regardless of their feelings about life as students, are still more likely to be leftist than either satisfied or dissatisfied non–

liberal arts students. There does not seem to be any consistent relationship between satisfaction-dissatisfaction and being rightist. However, when political party preference is used as an indicator, the satisfied student is more likely than his dissatisfied peer to be on the right of the political spectrum. It should be remembered, though, that the dissatisfied students constitute only about one-quarter of the students.

Student satisfaction-dissatisfaction was also related to political activity as measured by voting in school elections and participation in demonstrations. This was done in order to ascertain whether the student dissatisfied with life as a student would be more likely than his more contented peer either to withdraw from campus political activity or to try to change the campus situation to bring it more in accord with his desires. Data not shown here indicate that he does not withdraw and is more likely than the satisfied student to participate in political activity. Fifty-six percent of the dissatisfied students voted in their school election, compared with 39 percent of the others. This relationship held when school was introduced as a control factor. And again, the dissatisfied student is almost twice as likely as the satisfied student to participate in demonstrations.

UNIVERSITY GRADE AVERAGE

A widespread belief exists among many academic persons that a relationship exists between intelligence and radicalism and activism among students anywhere. Although this hypothesis has not been submitted to careful study in most instances, the data are available with respect to the students at Berkeley. In 1957 two sociologists found that the brighter students, as measured by grade point average, were more likely to be highly libertarian than students with lower grade point averages. Eight years later, at the time of demonstrations at Berkeley, studies revealed a positive relationship between intelligence and both participation in and support for the student demonstrations. One survey of the student body revealed that 45 percent of the respondents with grade point averages of $B+$ or better could be classified as militant and only 10 percent as conservative. Among those with a $B-$ or less average, over one-third were conservatives, whereas 15 percent were militants.[46] According to another study, supporters of FSM (Free Speech Movement) at all class levels had higher grade point averages and were likely to have stronger intellectual orientations than the nonsupporters.[47] Among those arrested in the Sproul Hall sit-in of December 3, more than half of the undergraduates had a *B* average or better.[48]

Does the same situation exist at the University of Puerto Rico? In order to determine if an association existed between intelligence and student politics, university grade average was related to the student's politics and political activity. Before continuing with the analysis, however, we must admit that grades and grade point average are not necessarily the best indicators of intelligence. There are many factors that can intervene between intelligence and its expression through grades. There appear to be few who will accept any indicator of intelligence as being valid (including standard I.Q. tests). However, in the absence of a superior indicator, university grade average will be used in this case as a measure of intelligence with the knowledge that it is at best an imperfect measure.

In Table 49, the data reveal that such a relationship does exist. The higher the grade average of the student, the more likely he is to identify himself as leftist. Conversely, as university grade average declines, the percentage of students who consider themselves rightist increases. The proportion of students considering themselves leftist is highest among the best students, whereas the proportion identifying themselves as rightist is highest among those with the lowest grade average. When political party preference is used as a political indicator, the data show a similar relationship. As grade average improves, the percentage choosing the PIP steadily increases from 19 percent of the average students to 36 percent of the best students. As in Table 50, preference for the PER

---

46 Sommers, "Mainsprings of the Rebellion," p. 544.

47 Paul Heist, "Intellect and Commitment: The Faces of Discontent," Center for the Study of Higher Education, University of California, Berkeley, 1966 (mimeo), p. 22.

48 Sommers, "Mainsprings of the Rebellion," p. 544.

TABLE 49
University Grade Average and Student's Politics

Student's Political Position	University Grade Average		
	Average %	Good %	Best %
Left	12	26	35
Center	48	46	41
Right	40	28	24
Total	100	100	100
	=144	=250	=75
Student's Party Preference	%	%	%
PIP	19	27	36
PPD	53	43	44
PER	26	28	18
PAC	2	2	2
Total	100	100	100
	=152	=254	=72

and PAC, the conservative parties, increases as grade average declines.

At this point, the student's school was introduced in order to ascertain whether it had a cumulative, an independent, or any effect at all. As seen in Table 50, school has a differential effect. Among liberal arts students, the brighter the student the more likely he is to be leftist. Almost half of the brightest liberal arts students consider themselves on the left. Also, as university grade average declines among the liberal arts students, the percentage of self-identified rightist students increases. However, there is no clear relationship between university grade average and relative political position among the non–liberal arts students. One similarity between this group and liberal arts students is revealed in the political positions of the average non–liberal arts students. Like their liberal arts counterparts, the average non–liberal arts students are the least likely to be leftist and the most likely to be rightist.

The introduction of school as an added variable, however, weakens the relationship between intelligence and political party preference (Table 51). The relationship is neither clear nor consistent for either the liberal arts or non–liberal arts students. The data do reveal, though, that among the liberal arts students the best are most likely to prefer the PIP (51%) and least likely to prefer the PPD and the PER. Among the non–liberal arts students, the best student is least likely to favor the parties on the right of the political spectrum, although preference for the PIP is fairly similar for each of the three grade average groups. Thus, school makes less

TABLE 50
Influence of University Grade Average and School on Student's Political Position

	Grade Average					
	Average		Good		Best	
	Liberal	Non– Liberal	Liberal	Non– Liberal	Liberal	Non– Liberal
Student's Political Position	Arts %	Arts %	Arts %	Arts %	Arts %	Arts %
Left	31	5	36	17	48	14
Center	33	53	34	56	33	55
Right	36	42	30	27	19	31
Total	100	100	100	100	100	100
	=39	=105	=119	=131	=46	=29

TABLE 51
*Influence of University Grade Average and School
on Student's Party Preference*

	University Grade Average					
	Average		Good		Best	
	Liberal	Non– Liberal	Liberal	Non– Liberal	Liberal	Non– Liberal
Student's Party Preference	Arts %	Arts %	Arts %	Arts %	Arts %	Arts %
PIP	40	12	40	17	51	14
PPD	38	58	36	49	30	66
PER	17	30	24	31	19	17
PAC	5	1	—	3	—	3
Total	100	101*	100	100	100	100
	=40	=112	=116	=138	=43	=29

TABLE 52
Desired School Changes and University Grade Average

| | University Grade Average | | |
Desired Changes	Average %	Good %	Best %
Practical training and facilities	67	69	73
Academic freedom and participation in university government	33	31	27
Total	100	100	100
	=135	=220	=70

clear the relationship between intelligence and political position. However, the outlines of the relationship still exist; the brighter students are more likely to be leftist and the average students are more likely to be rightist. This trend has been recognized elsewhere. A study of American social scientists in universities during the McCarthy era found that the more productive the social scientist in terms of publications, the more likely he was to be permissive or liberal.[49]

One other measure of political position was employed, the most important changes the respondent would like to see at his school. The responses were divided between those who wanted changes of a practical nature and those who wanted more academic freedom and participation in school and university government. It was thought that the leftist student would be most in favor of more academic freedom and greater student participation in school government. When university grade average is related to desired school changes (Table 52), the data reveal only a slight relationship between intelligence and desired school change. The slight relationship that does exist indicates that the better the student, the less likely he is to favor political and academic changes. The introduction of the student's school, however, has an important impact upon the relationship between intelligence and desired school changes (Table 53). Among liberal arts students, there

[49] Paul Lazarsfeld and Wagner Thielens, Jr., *The Academic Mind: Social Scientists in a Time of Crisis*, pp. 144–145.

ceases to be any consistent relationship; about 40 percent of those in each grade category favor changes expanding student political participation and academic freedom. However, among non–liberal arts students, as university grade average increases, the percentage of students desiring more academic freedom and student participation decreases. Whereas 33 percent of the average students favor greater academic freedom and student participation, only 4 percent of the best students take this position.

The above data strongly suggest that school and intelligence mutually reinforce each other for liberal arts students and accentuate the students' predisposition to take a leftist position. The situation is not as clear for non–liberal arts students, since at times the two variables, intelligence and school, seem to work at cross-purposes.

Does intelligence affect the student's political activity as well as his political position? As seen in Table 54, the brighter the student, the more likely he is to have a great deal of interest in student politics. On the other hand, as university grade average declines, the more likely the student is to have little or no interest in student politics. When the respondent's school was introduced, however,

TABLE 53
Desired School Changes by School and University Grade Average

| | Grade Average | | | | | |
| | Average | | Good | | Best | |
Desired Changes	Liberal Arts %	Non–Liberal Arts %	Liberal Arts %	Non–Liberal Arts %	Liberal Arts %	Non–Liberal Arts %
Practical training and facilities	59	65	63	75	58	96
Academic freedom and participation in university government	41	35	37	25	42	4
Total	100 =34	100 =101	100 =105	100 =115	100 =43	100 =27

TABLE 54

Interest in Student Politics and University Grade Average

Interest in Student Politics	University Grade Average		
	Average %	Good %	Best %
Much	17	24	32
Some	43	44	39
Little or none	40	32	29
Total	100	100	100
	=156	=259	=76

TABLE 55

Interest in Student Politics by School and University Grade Average

	Grade Average					
	Average		Good		Best	
	Liberal Arts %	Non– Liberal Arts %	Liberal Arts %	Non– Liberal Arts %	Liberal Arts %	Non– Liberal Arts %
Interest						
Much	27	14	32	16	45	10
Some	45	42	44	44	36	45
Little or none	28	44	24	40	19	45
Total	100	100	100	100	100	100
	=40	=114	=120	=139	=47	=29

the relationship proved inconsistent (Table 55). Among the non–liberal arts students, the association between intelligence and interest in student politics virtually disappeared. The relationship between university grade average held only for the liberal arts students.

Next, political activity was considered to see the extent to which activity as opposed to interest might be related to intelligence. The data in Table 56 reveal, with one exception, a positive and consistent relationship between intelligence and activity for both liberal arts and non–liberal arts students. Within each school grouping, the brighter the student, the more likely he is to vote, to attend a meeting of the student council, and to hold a position of responsibility in a student organization. The one exception to this pattern is in the case of participation in demonstrations. Thus intelligence is positively related to increased political activity.

CONCLUSION

The climate at the University of Puerto Rico differs in many ways from that of universities in other parts of Latin America. The political activity of the students is limited, and, of those who are politically committed, the right appears to be a larger group than the left. The leftist students ordinarily are enrolled in the Schools of Social Sciences, Humanities, and Law. The rightist students come primarily from the Schools of Engineering, Business, and Natural Sciences. It is difficult to tell whether this division is predominantly a function of certain political types selecting a particular field of study, or whether particular fields of study produce certain political types (selection or socialization).

The division in the political attitudes of the students can be partially attributed to differences in the nature of the subject matter

TABLE 56
University Grade Average by School by Political Activity

	Grade Average					
	Average		Good		Best	
	Liberal Arts	Non–Liberal Arts	Liberal Arts	Non–Liberal Arts	Liberal Arts	Non–Liberal Arts
Activity	%	%	%	%	%	%
Voted	37	28	70	29	83	44
	=30	=96	=115	=112	=41	=23
Attended meeting of student council	25	22	50	24	52	38
	=40	=111	=117	=138	=44	=29
Held position in a student group	25	27	38	29	49	33
	=40	=111	=119	=136	=47	=30
Participated in demonstrations	25	20	31	18	28	23
	=40	=113	=119	=137	=46	=30

pursued in the schools. The liberal arts schools are oriented toward the study of man, his values, and his social relationships, whereas the non–liberal arts schools are far less oriented in this direction. It may also be that students in the social sciences and the humanities are exposed to ideas and ideologies that diverge from the dominant ideology of the Puerto Rican society. Their counterparts in the non–liberal arts fields pursue subject matter not overtly concerned with political ideology and giving little cause to question the ideology and assumptions underlying Puerto Rico's political position. Non–liberal arts students are being exposed to a professional orientation that narrows their focus in toward the discipline and a specific career. In addition, they are acquiring professional training that will enable them to reap the rewards of an acquisitive society almost immediately upon graduation. Thus they are less likely to question or actively oppose the status quo than the liberal arts students, whose schooling gives them a wider and different perspective on their society and few guarantees of its rewards. The differing political attitudes and behavior of the teaching staffs of the liberal and non–liberal arts schools may also contribute to the students' political differences. Teachers in the former tend to be more leftist and more politically active.

Student satisfaction and university grade average are also related to both political position and political activity. The more intelligent and the more dissatisfied student tends to be further left as well as more active than other students. However, the most important factor in determining political position and activity of the student was his school. University grade average and dissatisfaction with life as a student are secondary to the nature of his field of study in their effect on his politics. To reiterate, students in the liberal arts schools, compared with those in the non–liberal arts schools, are disproportionately more leftist and more politically active.

Chapter V

FUPI
The Militant Leftists

As mentioned previously, the climate and the regulations of the University of Puerto Rico tend to discourage political activity in general and political activity of a highly partisan nature in particular. Nonetheless, several student political organizations do exist, although their membership is generally quite limited. These organizations range from the leftist FUPI (University Federation for Independence) to the rightist FAU (University Federation of Anti-Communists). These two groups are the most important in terms of numbers and influence, although it is generally conceded that, of the two, FUPI has the larger membership and the greater influence. In between are the CPC (Christian Patriotic Crusade), Society of Friends of the People, and AUPE (University Association for Statehood).[1] These organizations can be divided politically between those who favor independence and those who desire statehood. FUPI, the CPC, and the Friends of the People have a proindependence orientation; AUPE and FAU stand for statehood.

FUPI is the only militant left-wing organization on the Río Piedras campus. FUPI members are nearly stereotypes of the pop-

NOTE: This chapter is based primarily on data gathered from interviews with members of FUPI, the University Federation for Independence. Interview data from other students and UPR faculty and administrators are also used. All interviews were conducted during the summer of 1965.

[1] Since the writing of this chapter, FAU appears to have submerged its identity and become the driving force behind AUPE.

ular conception of the typical Latin American student activist. To the extent that they resemble this prototype, they are deviants on the campus.

Although it has the largest membership of any student political organization, the number of FUPI students probably does not exceed three hundred. It is difficult to discern with any accuracy the exact size of FUPI. This organization has a continual student turnover and is lax about maintaining records. Its opponents claim that it has an active membership of only sixty, but its supporters assert that it numbers about two thousand. More objective interviewees have estimated FUPI's membership as about three hundred active members with sixty to one hundred of these forming the hard core.

Because the practical orientation of the University of Puerto Rico has led the upper class to send its children outside the island for their higher education, the student left has been deprived of a pool from which leaders and nationalist students might have emerged. Since the founding of the university, the upper class has not been adequately represented within the student body. In other countries of Latin America, the students of elitist universities, primarily, have spearheaded radical movements. Students concerned with the problems of making a living are not as free as an elite to engage in radical activities. The leftists and the nationalists at the University of Puerto Rico have suffered from a lack of students who, motivated by a sense of noblesse oblige and characterized by a disdain for material gains, might have made FUPI not only larger in numbers, but also more influential.

In addition, the students who have studied abroad have generally not attended schools that would predispose them to encourage leftist-nationalist movements upon their return to the island. Students from the French and British colonial possessions have attended such schools as the London School of Economics or the University of Paris, where they have come in contact with strong left-wing movements and faculty members oriented toward socialism, like Professor Harold Laski. Puerto Rican students attending Harvard, Columbia, or the University of Chicago (at the time of this study) have not had similar contacts or experiences.

Despite these handicaps, FUPI has an impact that far exceeds its size. Everyone interviewed, whether friend or foe of FUPI, marvelled at the dedication and the amount of time and energy that FUPI members devote to political activity. Few political or administrative measures affecting the students are planned without taking FUPI into account. For example, when a leading administrative official was asked to explain the absence of a student newspaper, he answered that the chancellor and the administration truly desired to reinstate the newspaper, but did not dare because of FUPI. "A student newspaper needs an editorial board. Who would control this editorial board? A political group, and most likely it would be FUPI. This could not be permitted." Thus, due to fear of FUPI, the university has remained without a student newspaper.

When FUPI takes a stand on an issue, the entire university community, up to and including Chancellor Benítez, measures its own response thereby. The very existence of FAU, FUPI's mortal enemy, is a reaction to FUPI. Supporters and members of FAU asserted that FAU has only one reason for existence—opposition to FUPI and to communism, which to FAU members are one and the same.

FUPI, despite its size, appears to be moving to a position where it will set the tone to which many will conform and to which all will react. There are very few universities in Latin America or elsewhere where the major portion of the student body is composed of militant activists. The ability of a small but articulate minority to give the impression of speaking for an entire student generation has been noted by observers in the United States. Today, when students have come alive politically, Martin Meyerson, the former acting chancellor at Berkeley, estimates that the student activists constitute only about 2 percent of the university students in the United States. The other 98 percent have been and continue to remain "silent."[2] David Riesman has pointed out that, even during the depression thirties in the United States, student radicals re-

[2] *Time*, September 9, 1966, p. 46.

mained a minority. Nonetheless, "at some institutions they, along with their faculty mentors, helped set the tone to which other students conformed."[3]

To see more clearly how a system normally operates, it is often fruitful to view that system during a period of strain or crisis. Similarly, the analysis of deviant cases enlarges understanding of norms, because by shedding light on reasons for deviation, such analysis also sheds light on conformity. Lipset, Coleman, and Trow's study of the International Typographical Union, for example, has revealed not only why it is a democratic union, but also why the majority of unions are not democratic.[4] FUPI members are deviants in regard to the campus and society, not only in the statistical sense, but also in their frequent violation of university norms and regulations. If we can gain some insight into the processes operative among FUPI members, it may help us to understand the vast majority of students who are neither politically active nor politically left.

FUPI was organized in 1956. In its constitution, FUPI claimed to be the direct successor to the General Council of Students that was dissolved in 1948 during the student demonstrations. Thus FUPI is not just a political organization representing one particular point of view; it claims to be the one student government representing all students. Its own organizational structure mirrors that of the university, since it too is organized by faculties. As the student government, FUPI expects the support of all the students.

As a political organization, FUPI has committed itself to two basic objectives: (1) to defend the Puerto Rican student, which includes the establishment of university autonomy, democracy within the university, and university *co-gobierno* among faculty, students, and professors; and (2) to struggle against colonialism until Puerto Rico is free. Its secondary objectives are the abolition of militarism, racism, political persecution, and social injustice, as well as the defense of Puerto Rican history and national culture.

[3] David Riesman, "The Influence of Student Culture and Faculty Values in the American College," *Higher Education: The Yearbook of Education, 1959*, p. 387.
[4] Seymour M. Lipset, Martin Trow, and James Coleman, *Union Democracy*.

Any student who believes in student democracy and independence for Puerto Rico is eligible for membership in FUPI. No one will be barred because of political philosophy, party membership, or religion. FUPI claims to be free of any particular political philosophy and subordinate to no organization. According to FUPI's statement of principles, "FUPI is neither Marxist, Catholic, Protestant, or social democratic. FUPI is a nonpartisan student organization concerned with democracy and patriotism."[5]

Although it is neither subordinate to nor affiliated with any insular party, FUPI seems to be allied with the MPI (Proindependence Movement). Students who drop out or graduate are advised to join the MPI. In numerous instances of picketing and demonstrating, FUPI and MPI have coordinated their activities. A recent example of cooperation was the electoral boycott campaign of 1964. Despite this close cooperation, FUPI members strongly insist that they are independent of outside control.

The informal requirements for membership in FUPI are the ability to work hard and the willingness to put in long hours for the organization. FUPI members are continually active both on and off campus. They frequently hold rallies near the campus, and pickets are sent to support striking workers or MPI demonstrators. Approximately once a week, FUPI's mimeograph machine churns out a newsletter to be distributed at the entrances to the campus. In addition, FUPI participates in island election campaigns and launches its own campaigns to support such issues as university reform. Meetings are held frequently to plot strategy and to distribute work assignments. Such a schedule leaves the FUPI member little time for anything else, including his studies. Several members of FUPI who were interviewed castigated themselves because of their inability or lack of desire to work long and hard for FUPI. They felt that they were less worthy than the real activists.

Despite the open door and noble proclamations, FUPI members constitute only about 2 percent of the student body at Río Piedras. According to the survey data, however, 23 percent of the students

[5] The Executive Committee of FUPI, ed., "¿Qué es la FUPI?" (mimeo), p. 4.

favor independence. This implies that FUPI has been unsuccessful in recruiting, not only from the general student body, but even from students sympathetic to independence. Why?

For the militants within FUPI, the answer to the question is simple. Students do not become members of FUPI because they are afraid. What do they have to fear? When interviewed, every member of FUPI mentioned harassment by the FBI and the police. As mentioned earlier, each FUPI student told of FBI visits to his parents, his parents' neighbors, his father's employers, and his own employer as well. During the course of the visit, the FBI agent warns of the dangers of membership in an organization like FUPI. As a consequence of FBI visits, FUPI members have lost jobs and have been subjected to pleas from their parents to leave FUPI. The FBI and the police frequently photograph FUPI members when they gather in "their corner" of the university cafeteria, as well as when they are demonstrating and picketing.

FUPI members also claim that the university discriminates against them. They are either not hired by the university or, if they are hired, they are quickly fired. Many FUPI students asserted that the university was unfair to them in its distribution of scholarships. In response to the administration claim that a large proportion of FUPI has scholarships, FUPI leaders replied that most had these scholarships before they joined FUPI.

Whether or not these charges are true, many non-FUPI students believe that they are. In addition, some students sympathetic to FUPI claimed that their concern over employment opportunities after graduation or their desire to enter a good graduate or professional school has prevented them from joining FUPI. The president of FUPI, a recent graduate from the School of Social Sciences, claimed that he was having difficulty obtaining satisfactory employment. He wanted to attend Law School, but he thought that his politics would probably bar his admission.

The general attitude toward FUPI, both within the university and outside it, has given the organization a negative stigma. Newspapers and radio stations constantly refer to FUPI as an agent of Moscow or Castro. When people outside the campus were asked about FUPI, most asserted that, as a matter of proven fact, FUPI members were Communists. There is consequently much hostility toward FUPI. For example, one FUPI student said that after he mentioned that he belonged to FUPI, his date's father kicked him down a flight of stairs.

FUPI leaders feel that this community hostility is a major reason why most students do not join FUPI until their junior year. According to its president, it takes FUPI two years to teach students that FUPI members neither have horns nor are Communist. FUPI has started a campaign, however, to orient students at the high school level.[6] If this succeeds, the student at the university will be a member of FUPI for all four years instead of the normal two. This would make for greater continuity; the organization constantly suffers the shock of two-year turnovers.

There is another side to the coin of FUPI's failure to recruit members. Technically, membership is open to all; in reality, it is not. How could it be in a vanguard organization? Potential supporters and proindependence students are repelled by FUPI's posture and positions. The image that FUPI presents is arrogantly revolutionary. Members seem to think that FUPI has a monopoly on the truth and that compromise is a betrayal of principle. In general, support is invited or accepted strictly on FUPI terms. For prospective members, sympathy for independence is a necessary but not a sufficient condition. FUPI is not simply for Puerto Rican independence. To become a member of FUPI is also to become a supporter of Castro, Mao, and other heroes of the far left. FUPI is also an ardent and perennial critic of anything done by the university administration, the island government, the United States, and NATO. Membership in FUPI is therefore an ideological commitment to the radical left. In a society that is virulently anti-Communist and strongly pro–United States and on a campus that is conservative, this is asking a great deal.

[6] The president of FUPI had himself been attracted to politics during his high school years by a teacher who took him to PIP meetings; thus FUPI represented a continuation of a process of politicization already underway by the time he entered the UPR.

FUPI's revolutionary or sectlike stance has caused a selection process among even its own members. Members who are neither able nor willing to work the long hours FUPI requires and those who have questioned FUPI's strong ideological position are relegated to second-class membership. The president of the student council in the School of Social Sciences considered himself a FUPI member, although not an active one. His activity in FUPI waned as he became more involved in his studies and as his desire to go to graduate school increased. At the same time, he began to question some of FUPI's policies, especially those linking Puerto Rican independence with support for socialism and Castro. However, he claimed that he still remained a member of FUPI and desired independence for Puerto Rico. When his name was brought up during an interview with FUPI leaders, they made it quite clear that they did not consider him a member of their organization. They thought that he had "sold out" when he started to think about his own immediate future. In FUPI there is no room for such people.

FUPI leaders were also asked to explain the ideological position of their organization. Not only the leaders, but virtually every FUPI member was surprised when asked, "Why are you in favor of independence?" The only response was that the Puerto Ricans are a people with a national heritage and culture and that as a people they are entitled to independence as a natural right. "Why were FUPI members able to come to this conclusion and not other students?" The others, according to FUPI members, also are for Puerto Rican independence. According to one FUPI student, even *estadistas*, when they were drunk at parties, would admit they were proindependence. But only FUPI members are able to rise above their fears and brainwashing. "Are you Socialist?" "No." "Why do you support Castro, Mao?" "We support them because they freed their peoples from foreign domination and not because they are Socialists or Communists." "Why are you anti–United States?" "Because the United States is the colonial oppressor and exploits us." "Why does the United States want Puerto Rico to remain a colony and how does it exploit you?" At this point, FUPI leaders ran into difficulty in answering. "The United States wants Puerto

Rico to remain a colony in order to extract profits from the Puerto Rican people." "But doesn't Puerto Rico have the highest standard of living in the Caribbean and in Latin America?" "Yes, but this would have been true without the United States." When asked about the larger numbers attending universities compared with other countries and about the extensive public housing and public health and welfare measures, FUPI leaders could not give meaningful responses. To them, these were inconsequential things that they had not seriously considered. "Does FUPI provide an analysis of how the United States is exploiting Puerto Rico or a program that documents how independence is to be achieved?" "No," the president declared. "At this point in time, such things are not needed. What is needed now is action. FUPI is involved in meetings, pickets, demonstrations, passing out leaflets, and collecting funds. Later there will be time for analyses. A few years ago, FUPI was nothing. Now, because of its activities, FUPI is feared and respected by many people, including faculty members and members of the administration."

FUPI is similar to a religious sect in many ways. Membership in it must be earned. Its view of the world is a simple one: the world is divided between the forces of good and evil. Intellectual analysis is disregarded. The leadership and the activists of FUPI feel that it is their mission as keepers of the faith to spread it among the duped and the heathen. In order to do this, they are almost willing to sacrifice their lives and careers like the martyrs of old.

The major opposition to FUPI among the students is FAU. It came into existence in the 1963–1964 semester, when students with strong anti-Communist feelings picketed against the university's policy toward Professor Lima of the Mathematics Department. Professor Lima was hired while he was studying at Berkeley. On the way to Puerto Rico, he stopped and visited Cuba, and on his arrival in Puerto Rico publicly declared himself to be a Marxist-Leninist. The newspapers raised a hue and cry when Chancellor Benítez refused to fire him. Out of the furor surrounding this incident, FAU emerged. Like FUPI, FAU is basically a one-issue organization. Instead of seeking independence, FAU is dedicated to combatting communism. In FAU's view, FUPI members are all Communists, as are most of the faculty of the Schools of Social Science and Humanities and some of the members of the administration. FAU's activities are limited to denouncing FUPI, holding counterdemonstrations, and acting as counterpickets. The president of FAU has said, "It is necessary for us to be as hard as nails toward FUPI and crush them before they crush us." There have been several physical confrontations between FUPI and FAU members.[7]

FAU members do not work as hard for their organization as FUPI members do, nor is FAU membership as large as FUPI's. Estimates of FAU's membership run from 15 to 150. Nonetheless, some faculty members are convinced that on any given issue FAU would obtain more support than FUPI. The vote on the student referendum of March 26, 1965, concerning the regulation of student activities is a case in point. FAU opposed the extension of political activities among students, whereas FUPI was in favor. As mentioned previously, the students defeated it by a two-to-one margin.

There are also differences between the two organizations' sources of recruitment. FAU's membership is derived primarily from the School of Business; FUPI members are primarily students in the Schools of Social Science and Humanities. Interestingly, the School of Business seems a stronger base of support for FAU than does the School of Social Science for FUPI. On the referendum, the School of Business voted overwhelmingly for the restricted FAU position, but the School of Social Science supported FUPI's liberal stand by only a very slim margin. Furthermore, in 1964 students in the School of Business elected an active member of FAU as their

---

[7] In 1966 and 1967, there were repeated clashes between FUPI and AUPE members. Police were called onto the campus and students were suspended. These clashes have further polarized the campus community. However, the traditional apathy of the vast majority has continued. One indicator of this is the student turnout in the elections for student councils of the various schools. Less than 5 percent of the humanities students voted; the comparable percentage at the School of Social Sciences and School of Natural Sciences was 19 percent and 11 percent respectively (*San Juan Star*, December 10, 1967).

student council president by a comfortable majority. An inactive FUPI member, after several defeats, was narrowly elected student council president of the School of Social Sciences.

The most vociferous support and some of the most active members of FAU are Cuban exiles, for example, the president of the student council of the School of Business. Like their older counterparts, they are militantly anti-Communist and ardent foes of independence for Puerto Rico. FAU and its Cuban refugee supporters are strongly pro–United States and are champions of statehood for Puerto Rico. FAU members have attended meetings of Young Republicans in the United States and were ardent supporters of Barry Goldwater in the United States' 1964 election.

It was difficult to obtain information about the social-class origins of either FUPI or FAU. Most members of FUPI who were available for interviews thought that their membership consisted of predominantly middle-class students, with a sprinkling of poorer and wealthier students. The FUPI members who came from well-to-do homes felt that FUPI had a fair number of wealthier students, and not too many poorer FUPI members disagreed. Among the activists who were interviewed, including the president, backgrounds were a mixture of middle and working classes. The president said he had emerged from the proletariat and was proud of it. Most of the very active FUPI members, again including the president, had in common the fact that they had come from broken homes. They had been brought up by their mothers; their fathers had either died or deserted the family. One student, who had not seen his father since he was six, stated dramatically, "My father got lost in the jungles of New York."

Another bond held in common by most FUPI members is a lack of religion. Not one of the students interviewed attended services regularly or considered himself devout. Most viewed themselves as atheists or agnostics. FAU members, on the other hand, were regarded by the university community as ardent Catholics. FUPI members are not entirely hostile to the Church, since they are aware that some good Catholics favored independence. Father

Marguerito and the Crusadio Patriótica Cristiana are highly regarded for their proindependence activities among the peasantry. It is the Catholic hierarchy, FUPI members feel, that is "selling out" Puerto Rico to the United States.

FUPI members are universally respected on campus because of their intelligence. Friend and foe admitted that FUPI recruits the brightest students on the Río Piedras campus. One dean stated that as a group they have a high grade average and a disproportionate number of scholarship holders. On the other hand, FAU members are not noted for their intelligence. They have a reputation among their sympathizers, as well as among their enemies, of substituting emotion for thought. Although sympathetic to the FAU movement, one dean stated, "Members of FAU are probably out of their heads."

The administration's attitude toward FUPI and FAU seems to be a mixture of hostility and Machiavellianism. On the one hand, it is not pleased with any group of students that is a potential source of difficulty, especially difficulty of a political nature. FUPI is the biggest thorn in the administration's side, since it is forever challenging campus regulations and making demands. Although FAU is not highly regarded by the administration, it is looked upon as a useful counterweight to FUPI. Demands for a campus-wide student council were dismissed on the grounds that the students were too divided to agree on a student council. FAU and FUPI have been played off against each other to maintain the status quo and to prevent FUPI from making greater inroads.

The concern over FUPI and its activities is continually voiced by administration personnel. Why should this be so? After all, the administrators themselves have stated that the FUPI activists number only about sixty in an overall population of more than eighteen thousand students. One dean tried to account for this concern. He felt that of these eighteen thousand students, about twelve thousand (or two out of three), really do not care about anything. The remaining six thousand, he claimed, are concerned enough to give their support on issues they deem important. FUPI and FAU, then, can be viewed as vying for the loyalties of these six thousand students. The administration realizes that a small, dedicated group of intelligent activists, such as FUPI, might be able to make some sizable headway into this group. Thus the administration is anxious to prevent FUPI from gaining popularity among the students.

An alternative analysis of FUPI's gaining support among the students also seems cogent. The administration, through design or otherwise, has encouraged many of the divisions that exist on the campus. The faculty is not only divided by their loyalties to their own schools, but is split into pro- and anti-Benítez camps as well. The students are also divided. Students from different faculties rarely have an opportunity to interact meaningfully with one another. The student councils exist for each individual school and are oriented toward the problems of that school. Until 1966 a campus-wide student council was prohibited by university regulations. The only central authority for the entire campus is the chancellor, who also governs the administration quite efficiently. Furthermore, the administration is the only legitimate campus-wide organization. Although neither FUPI nor FAU is recognized by the administration, FUPI is the only other organization that can compete with the administration. It too is campus-wide, is efficiently operated, and has a strong central authority. FUPI is the only organized opposition to the administration that crosses the parochial barriers of schools. In this sense, FUPI is filling a vacuum that the chancellor helped to create by banning the General Council of Students and eliminating the school newspaper. As Marx has pointed out, one condition necessary for the emergence of class consciousness is facile communication among members of that class. Although there are over eighteen thousand students at the Río Piedras campus, communication among them is obstructed by particularistic school ties. FUPI has the potential to become a communications nexus that would unite many of the students into a genuine campus community. Thus concern with FUPI by the administration is well grounded. However, FUPI's ability to realize this potential has been hampered by its own sometimes arrogant attitude, by university regulations, and by campus apathy. Until 1964, the administration's fears that its various faculty opponents and non-FUPI student dissidents might make common cause with FUPI were exaggerated.

In October of 1964, several events simultaneously occurred that resulted in a coalition among FUPI, the movement for university reform, anti-Benítez professors, and many students who had not previously been active in politics. The Puerto Rican campaign for governor was underway. FUPI, allied with the MPI, was vigorously campaigning for an electoral boycott to show to the world Puerto Rico's true status as a colony. At the same time, other students and some faculty members were ardently working for university reform. They desired an academic upgrading of the university, competitive hiring of professors on the basis of ability, and, most important, the reduction of the nearly absolute power of the chancellor. Anti-Benítez faculty were utilizing the reform movement as a means of attacking Chancellor Benítez.

FUPI was also interested in university reform. The president of FUPI said, in language reminiscent of Berkeley's Mario Savio, that his organization favored it because "the university should cease to be a place for indoctrination, preparing people to be cogs in the wheels of machines." He too was in favor of improving the academic standards of the university. But FUPI's idea of university reform went beyond that held by other students. FUPI wanted the university to concern itself with the "real" issues of Puerto Rico, particularly the status issue. FUPI also favored *co-gobierno* among professors, students, and administration. Another FUPI activist put it much more bluntly. He felt that FUPI was willing to work with any other group in order to promote university reform. FUPI's interest in reform, according to him, was primarily political. "Once there is freedom and democracy within the university, FUPI would then be allowed to have a university forum. This would facilitate the recruitment of new members, the influencing of others, and the radicalization of the university. Once this occurs, the university could be used as a lever to change the entire society."

FUPI's position, needless to say, had very few supporters on campus. However, in the midst of the campaigns for electoral boycott and for university reform, an event took place that united various other campus elements with FUPI. On October 27, two FUPI hecklers at a FAU rally were hit and injured by some FAU supporters. In protest, FUPI scheduled a rally for the next day. In violation of university regulations, FUPI members marched through campus, urging everyone to attend. The administration summoned the police to the campus and ordered the marchers to leave. When a stalemate developed, the FUPI members sat down and several hundred other students began to gather around them. The police lost their patience and charged into the students, injuring several. Some observers claimed that the non-FUPI students received the brunt of the police attack. In response to the police charge, the students rapidly dispersed and spread the news throughout the campus. Soon students were throwing stones at the police, and the police began to use tear gas and to fire their guns into the air. During the course of the evening, several police cars were burned and eleven students were arrested. Calm was eventually restored with the assistance of Juan Maris Bras, the secretary general of the MPI, who seventeen years earlier had been expelled from the same campus for leading student demonstrations. Chancellor Benítez blamed the disturbances on professional political agitators associated with MPI efforts to organize the electoral boycott. He ordered the university closed until November 5, two days after the election. The campuses at Mayagüez and Humacao were also closed when the students became restive. *El Mundo*, the largest circulating newspaper, blamed the Communists and other subversive elements for causing the disturbances. A PER spokesman claimed, "It shows that there is a danger of Communism to higher education in Puerto Rico."

The events of October 28 united and mobilized the campus. FUPI, for once, had a sympathetic image as an underdog subjected to police brutality. The proponents of university reform and other students and faculty angry at the presence and conduct of the police on campus joined with FUPI in a protest march from the campus to the Capitol Building in Old San Juan on October 29. About five thousand students and faculty from all the schools, FUPI and non-FUPI students, supporters of reform, anti-Benítez elements, and nuns in clerical garb marched three hours to the governor's mansion. Pressure for reform was maintained, and the island legislature eventually passed legislation that, among other things, allowed for a campus-wide student government.[8]

FUPI, then, can be described as a small band of negativistic and embittered persons dedicated to the cause of Puerto Rican independence. FUPI, like its adult counterpart, the MPI, has neither developed an analysis of the situation as perceived by its membership nor established a carefully thought out program for achieving .ts goals. As a result, FUPI drifts from issue to issue, hoping fervently that the one issue may arise that will awaken the "drugged masses."

The quest appears quixotic. On the campus, almost three out of four students are children of fathers who lack college degrees. For most of them, the future means nonmanual jobs and the money to live at the level to which most of the island's population aspires. Outside the campus, a wide array of modern consumer goods from cars to television sets present a constant appeal. The standard of living has risen fairly steadily, and the economic future of the island looks bright. Against this background, what has FUPI to offer? To accept FUPI's view of the world and to become an active member of the left is to close the door to future economic and social rewards. It is no wonder that FUPI's appeals fall on deaf ears.

Why were even the small number of FUPI members willing to forego the benefits their society offers to holders of a college degree? What differentiates them from the vast majority of their college peers? FUPI members generally are not second-generation leftists socialized by frustrated radical parents to carry on the fight against

---

[8] The sources for the above include FUPI and non-FUPI students; faculty and administration personnel; the *New York Times*, October 29–30, 1964; *El Mundo*, October 28–30, 1964; *San Juan Star*, October 29–30, 1964.

the imperialist oppressor. In fact, most of their parents either are apolitical or support the PPD or the PER. Nor do FUPI members come from a minority group that has suffered real or imagined discrimination or persecution. The darker-skinned Puerto Rican student is not evident among the ranks of FUPI; traditionally, the darker-skinned Puerto Ricans have been ardent supporters of statehood for Puerto Rico. The members of FUPI are neither impoverished students, who might harbor resentment from real or imagined social injustice, nor wealthy students, who could pursue the quest for independence out of a sense of noblesse oblige. They are not modernists frustrated by the rule of traditionalists, nor are they traditionalists calling for the return of the old order.

FUPI members do differ from their classmates, however, in several ways. Generally, they are brighter than the others. Religion seems to play no role in their lives. FUPI members are more likely to be drawn from the Schools of Humanities and Social Sciences than from the other schools. In all these respects, FUPI members resembled those students in the survey who identified themselves as being to the left of their peers. One thing that seems to characterize the more militant activists, including the president, is the fact that the father had been absent from the home since childhood or early adolescence. Perhaps it is too facile to attribute their current rebellious activities, frequently directed against such father figures as Chancellor Jaime Benítez or former Governor Muñoz Marín, to the lack of a father in their own homes during the formative years. Despite the Freudian overtones of this interpretation, the relationship between the absence of the father and militant activity should not be discounted and perhaps warrants further research. The importance of the family in Puerto Rican culture was commented upon earlier.

A recurring theme in the interviews with FUPI students was the need or desire to establish an individual identity. Perhaps it is this need that differentiates FUPI members from other students. The responses to the query "Why are you for Puerto Rican independence?" reflect this need. To a man, the reply was that Puerto Ricans were a people, that as a people they had a unique cultural heritage and therefore merited an independent existence. Their strongest criticism against the United States focused on its cultural imperialism. Complaints about economic exploitation were sometimes added, almost as an afterthought. (The fear and hatred of Yankee suppression of their heritage expressed itself in an interesting manner. Most of the militants interviewed began their conversations with me in Spanish; only when I proved that I would converse in Spanish would they change to English. One of the most militant members interviewed spoke only in Spanish for an hour and then decided to change to fluent English.) The United States, FUPI members claimed, was trying to eradicate Puerto Rican culture and the identity of the Puerto Ricans as a people.

FUPI itself is a source of identity for its members. When asked about FUPI and its accomplishments, most pointed to its very existence and to the fact that many on the campus, including those in positions of power, feared or respected it. The fact that so few could cause so many such concern was a constant source of pride to FUPI members. FUPI students also seemed pleased that on such a large campus their activities had made them so well-known that almost all the students could recognize FUPI members on sight.

This desire to establish an individual identity can also be seen in career choices. All who were interviewed aspired to be either writers, lawyers, or professors. These professions are characterized by a great deal of individual autonomy combined with mandate for self-expression.

We have attempted to distinguish the student radicals from their less politically active peers and to document the difficulties of a group of militant, independence-oriented students in a situation where they are unable to attract much of a following. These militant students are generally brighter and less religious than other students, and most likely to be in the Schools of Social Science and Humanities. In addition, their need to express their identities differentiates them from their peers. Independence, their major issue, is not sufficiently attractive to obtain the support of upwardly mobile students concerned with jobs and material benefits. Nor is FUPI very interested in forming a broad coalition, in which it would be but one member. Its goals are specific, and its ideological stance is not very flexible. FUPI has managed to achieve a measure of success only when, through a series of fortunate coincidences, several factors have combined to produce widely based sympathy for its role in the university. Nevertheless, despite FUPI's general failure to realize its goal or to gain a mass base, the revolutionary ardor of this vanguard student organization has not yet been dampened.

Chapter VI

SUMMARY AND CONCLUDING REMARKS

For the most part, university students in Puerto Rico have failed to heed the call of either nationalism or left-wing radicalism. The left at the University of Puerto Rico, as measured by preference for the PIP and relative political position, is a minority of the student body. They are also numerically smaller than those students who support the PER and consider themselves on the right. The position that attracts the most support is the center, composed of those students who prefer the PPD and regard themselves as being in the middle of the political spectrum on the campus. This study has attempted to explain the reasons behind these different political positions.

The focus of attention has been primarily upon the leftist minority. How did they differ from their more conservative peers? Social class and residence while at college appear to make little difference in terms of differentiating the students' political positions. The principal difference between the leftist students and their classmates seems to be that (a) they tend to be less religious, (b) they tend to have the same politics as their fathers, (c) they tend to be brighter, (d) they tend to be more dissatisfied with their role as student, and (e) they tend to be disproportionately located within the Schools of Humanities, Social Sciences, and Law. It is also clear that differences in the nature of the university experience are the major factor in differentiating the leftist students from their peers.

Interviews with members of FUPI, the most militant leftist-nationalist group of students, reinforced the findings derived from the analysis of the questionnaires. One attribute most peculiar to the members of FUPI is the desire to find and express their identities. For them, militant nationalism and anti-Americanism as expressed through their membership in FUPI becomes the primary vehicle for the satisfaction of this need.

It was also necessary to examine the environment, historical and contemporary, of these Puerto Rican university students in order to understand their political attitudes. Throughout its history, one salient political fact distinguishes Puerto Rico from every other colonial dependency in Latin America. Puerto Rico has never had a full-scale revolt against either Spain or the United States. Furthermore, with the exception of a brief interlude during the 1930's, Puerto Rico has lacked a broadly based political movement dedicated to national independence. Today, the island proponents of independence are numerically very inferior to those who desire statehood. The left, as represented by the MPI, or even the PIP, is virtually nonexistent as a political force in Puerto Rico today.

Under both Spain and the United States, Puerto Rico has failed to develop strong indigenous institutions. Religious and educational institutions have been either weak or dominated by non–Puerto Rican personnel and values. Culturally, Puerto Rico has been inundated with American values and practices that are having a strong effect upon the value hierarchy of the Puerto Rican populace. The development of an independent Puerto Rican middle class has been hampered by non–Puerto Rican control and influence over the economy. Important political decisions affecting the status of the island have been made, from the time of Columbus until the present, by non–Puerto Ricans residing outside the island.

The nature of the university itself is an important factor in the underdevelopment of the left and student nationalism. Since its founding in 1903, the University of Puerto Rico has been oriented toward such practical subjects as business, engineering, and the training of public school teachers. Associated with this practical orientation has been the lack of a serious intellectual experience or exchange on the part of many students and faculty. Furthermore, the university has since 1940 aimed at increasing the enrollment and extending the advantages of a college education to segments of the lower-middle and working classes. It has so succeeded in this task that today Puerto Rico, in addition to having a heterogeneous student body, ranks high among the nations of the world in terms of the percentage of the college-age cohort attending school. Thus the student body consists mainly of students who are the first in their families to attend college. These upwardly mobile students, particularly those in the Schools of Business, Engineering, and Education, who represent the majority of the students, are concerned with acquiring the skills and the diploma that will enable them to obtain their share of the material benefits offered by an acquisitive society. The tone set by these students and by a university oriented toward practicality does not foster a concern for such abstractions as national identity or nationalism.

Largely because of this practical orientation, the upper class has been proportionately underrepresented in the student body since the founding of the University of Puerto Rico. This has had serious consequences on the nature of student politics at the University of Puerto Rico. It has meant that the left and the nationalists on the campus have been deprived of a class that has traditionally supplied leaders to student movements elsewhere in Latin America. Students from elitist backgrounds, freed to a great extent from the economic concerns that grip most of their peers, might have made the left on the campus of the University of Puerto Rico a more significant force.

Those students who are concerned with nationalism or with promoting a socialist society are confronted with a difficult situation. Not only are they a minority within the university, but also the society lying beyond the university gates is unlike other Latin American societies in which leftist-nationalist students have been able to exert an important influence. Until very recently, these societies have been those lacking any organized force except the army and the students. They have also tended to be characterized by unpopular or unstable governments and a slow rate of economic growth or improvement in the standard of living. In Puerto Rico, however, the government is stable and genuinely popular, as well as welfare oriented. From 1940 until 1968, the ruling party was the

PPD, an experienced and well-organized party that had shown few indications of seriously weakening. However, in 1968 it split, and the election was won by Luis Ferre at the head of his statehood party. This signified, in Puerto Rican terms, a shift to the right on the political spectrum. The standard of living has rapidly improved, and the steady growth of the economy has enabled college graduates to find positions that are related to their course of studies or that provide sufficient rewards to compensate for the time spent in college. An increasing number of persons on the island are experiencing a vicarious mobility through the purchase of television sets, cars, and cooperative apartments, and through sending their children to higher levels of schooling. Finally, behind these imposing roadblocks to the development of a strong leftist-nationalist movement stands the United States.

The student left as well as the nonstudent left in Puerto Rico appears to have little chance of gaining power in the present circumstances. At this historical juncture, the left is small and weak and has nothing concrete to offer a populace growing accustomed to increased material benefits. Instead of programs and analyses, it offers slogans. The call for nationalization of industry in Puerto Rico does not strike a responsive chord; objectively it appears quite unrealistic. As pointed out earlier, many Puerto Rican industries are either subsidiaries of mainland industries dependent upon parts and essential services, or else they are distributive outlets for United States corporations. How, for example, would one nationalize Sears Roebuck's Puerto Rican branches? The Puerto Rican left seems to be becoming increasingly ideological as its chances for success in the political marketplace decrease. Both the student and nonstudent left assume that political demonstrations and the repetition of the slogan "Puerto Rico for the Puerto Ricans" will eventually garner the mass support they so ardently desire.

The only chance that the radicals and nationalists have to gain power is in the event of a severe depression. Should the economy no longer be able to satisfy the occupational expectations of the college graduates or the material desires of the population at large, then, perhaps, there might be a mass rejection of the United States and a focusing of hostility outward instead of inward, which together would lead to the ascendance of leftist-nationalism on the island. Contemporary Puerto Rican students, the children of their fathers, have disproved a maxim that has characterized nationalist movements in many areas of the world. Puerto Ricans, including the students, have shown that man *can* live by bread alone.

EPILOGUE

During the last several months there have been militant pro-independence demonstrations, bombings, and other acts of violence associated with the struggle for independence in Puerto Rico. Young Puerto Ricans, particularly students and FUPI members, appear to constitute a significant proportion of the demonstrators. This gives rise to at least two questions. Have the Puerto Rican students become radicalized? What has sparked this increase in pro-independence militance and violence?

From all indications, it is only a minority of all students who are taking part in the violence and demonstrations. Those who do participate appear to be disproportionately drawn from the schools that have generally supplied the independence activists, namely the Schools of Social Science and Humanities at the University of Puerto Rico. If the Puerto Rican students were to be surveyed again today, I seriously doubt whether their political profile would differ significantly from that of 1964. But although these recent activists are a minority, I think that they are a growing minority, larger in size and more militant than student activists of a few years ago. Why?

There appear to be three major factors that have become more visible since 1964–1965 and that underlie the growing unrest in Puerto Rico. The defeat of the PPD in the 1968 gubernatorial election, although due to a split within the party, symbolized the demise of the commonwealth middle-ground position. The victory of Louis Ferre, a long-time proponent of statehood, has at the same time sharply recast the debate over the issue of the island's status. Increasingly, Puerto Ricans, including the students, are being forced to choose between two diametrically opposed solutions to the status problem—independence or statehood. As this polarization continues, the radicalization of the political community at both ends of the spectrum will grow.

Another factor is the seemingly never-ending Vietnam War, and the draft. Like their counterparts on the mainland, large segments of draft-age youth question the morality, the brutality, and the futility of the war. They object to being drafted to fight in such a struggle. For Puerto Ricans, there is a special character to the war. They view it as a foreign war, not relevant to the needs or interests of the Puerto Rican people. This resentment is heightened by the fact that Puerto Ricans are constitutionally denied any official representation at the level of government where policy concerning the war and the draft is implemented and executed. Each publicized case of draft resistance and the federal prosecution of the offender fosters a growing proindependence militancy among the Puerto Rican youth.

A third factor has been the Puerto Rican exposure to both the civil rights and black power movements and the student movement in the United States. The massive presence of the United States media in Puerto Rico has afforded the island's populace, again especially the younger Puerto Ricans, the opportunity to examine closely the themes and tactics of these movements. The youth considered the relevance of these movements for Puerto Rico and, as they did, began to employ similar methods, along with Puerto Rican variants of the American ideologies. In addition, cheap and rapid transportation between Puerto Rico and the mainland has facilitated contact between Puerto Rican students and American militants. The net result has been to embolden the Puerto Rican activists, particularly FUPI, to engage in more open and direct militant tactics.

These three factors appear to be the most significant in explaining the rise of militancy in Puerto Rico. Although the majority of Puerto Rican students do not participate in political activity, there are indications that this studentry, which for eighteen years prior to 1964 remained politically uninvolved, may, like their American counterparts, become increasingly politicized. Puerto Rican students, like students elsewhere, cannot remain quiescent in the face of disturbing political and social factors that intrude into their lives.

APPENDIXES

Appendix I
Methodological Appendix

Data Collection Procedure

Several sources of data were used in this study. The primary source was an interview schedule completed by 577 students at the Río Piedras campus of the University of Puerto Rico during the summer of 1964. A secondary source of data was depth interviews with activist students conducted during the summer of 1965. Selected faculty and members of the university administration provided information utilized in this study. Puerto Rican newspapers, journals, and governmental and university materials were also employed.

The Interview Schedule

The interview schedule used in 1964 was compiled by the staff of the Institute of International Studies of the University of California. The twenty-three–page questionnaire employed in Puerto Rico is essentially the same instrument that the Institute's Comparative National Development Project has used in studies of students in Brazil, Colombia, Mexico, and Panama. Several questions pertaining to the Puerto Rican situation have been added (see Appendix II). The schedule includes several major sections: family and educational background, political attitudes and experiences, attitudes and activities with respect to the university, occupations, family, society, and future.

The Sample

The students in the primary sample were from nine faculties or schools within the University of Puerto Rico: Business Administration (70), Education (95), Engineering (71), General Studies (60), Humanities (49), Law (96), Medicine (13), Natural Sciences (50), and Social Sciences (73). Within each faculty, a systematic sample from an alphabetic list provided by the Computer Center of the University of Puerto Rico was employed. It was hoped that for each faculty it would be possible to obtain from 50 to 125 respondents. Due to administrative problems and unforeseen difficulties, the minimum was not obtained in the School of Medicine. The numbers that were obtained do not represent the actual distribution of students among the nine faculties.

During the summer of 1965, the present researcher conducted depth interviews among student activists. As there were no reliable lists of activists available, the respondents were selected through personal contacts with students and faculty members. Virtually all were members of FUPI (University Federation for Independence), a radical student organization.

English Version of Puerto Rican University Student Questionnaire

(INCLUDING THE DISTRIBUTION OF RESPONSES)

Institute of International Studies Comparative
National Development Project
Berkeley, California

This is a scientific study of public opinion concerning the problems of the university in general and of student life in particular. The study is essentially a comparative one, including more than fifteen universities in several Latin American nations, among them Brazil, Colombia, Mexico, and Panama. A central focus of the study is the adequacy of educational structures for fulfilling the needs of developing nations. The present study concentrates on a description by university students of their problems, both educational and other. By this means we hope to obtain a clear picture of university life, including its social, economic, political, and psychological aspects. The study is absolutely anonymous, and for this reason we request that you do not write in your name or any other indication of your identity as an individual. We are interested solely in frequencies and statistical tendencies, not in individual cases.

We request that you draw a circle around the number corresponding to your answer to each question (except for cases where a written answer is appropriate). Thus, in the first question, if you are 20 years old, circle the number 2, as below:

1. How old are you?
   Less than 18   1
   19 to 20   ②
   21 to 22   3

We request that you answer all the questions. There will be some in which the alternative answers provided may not precisely correspond to your opinion. In these cases, circle the response closest to your opinion, adding your comments on the reverse side of the page. The responses will be transferred to IBM cards, and statistical tables will be developed from them. The results of the study will be widely published in sociological journals.

[The percentages have been added to represent the distribution of responses by Puerto Rican students in the sample. In some cases the percentages will not total 100, because of rounding off or multiple responses. In the case of rounding off, it will be indicated by an asterisk (*), of multiple response, by a double asterisk (**).]

1. How old are you?

	%
18 or younger	17
19 to 20	38
21 to 22	22
23 to 24	8
25 to 26	5
27 to 30	3
31 to 35	3
36 to 40	2
More than 40	1

2. Are you male or female?

	%
Male	57
Female	43

3. What is the highest level of education your father, mother, and father's father received?

	Father %	Mother %	Father's Father* %
Primary school (complete or incomplete), or no education	21	27	28
Secondary school, general or *bachillerato* (complete or incomplete)	19	20	11
Secondary technical school (complete or incomplete)	22	23	8
Industrial or commercial institute (complete or incomplete)	3	7	1
University, incomplete	10	5	3
University, complete	23	16	7
Don't know	1	1	36
(No answer)	1	—	7

4. If your father, mother, or father's father attended university, whether or not they completed their studies, what was their field of specialization? (If more than one, indicate the most important.)

	Father*	Mother	Father's Father
	%	%	%
Did not attend university	67	79	90
Law	6	—	2
Medicine or other medical specialties (dentistry, veterinary medicine, nursing)	3	2	2
Social sciences (sociology, psychology, economy)	1	1	—
Humanities and fine arts (philosophy, literature)	1	3	—
Natural sciences (geology, agronomy, chemistry) and exact sciences (mathematics, physics)	1	1	—
Engineering (civil, chemical, electric)	7	0	1
Business administration, secretarial	7	4	1
Sciences of education (pedagogy)	4	7	1
Other	3	2	1
Don't know	1	1	2

5. Where did you live the major part of the time between the ages of seven and fifteen, and where did your father live the major part of the time up to the age of twenty-five?

	You lived from 7 to 15 years of age in: *	Your father lived up to the age of 25 in:
	%	%
San Juan	44	25
Mayagüez	4	6
Ponce	3	5
Humacao	1	2
City outside of Puerto Rico	5	6
City of more than 50,000 in Puerto Rico	5	5
City of 20,000 to 50,000 inhabitants in Puerto Rico	11	11
A city of less than 20,000 inhabitants in Puerto Rico	13	19
A town, farm, or rural zone	13	18
(No answer)	—	3

(a) In what department was it located
(where you lived)?   _____

(b) In what department was it located
(where your father lived)?   _____

6. What is your marital status?

	%
Single	81
Engaged	6
Married	12
Other (separated, divorced, widowed)	1

7. Do you have a job?
(a) How many hours a week do you work?

	%
I don't have a job	78
40 hours a week or more	10
20 to 39 hours per week	4
Less than 20 hours per week	2
(No answer)	6

(b) If you have a job, in what occupation do you work? (Please
provide details, including the level of specialization and level of
responsibility. Write freely in the space below. For example, "I
operate a grocery store, with four employees under my super-
vision.")

(c) Give a description of your work during an ordinary, typical
workday.

(d) Do you have subordinates, or persons that work under your
direction? How many?*

	%
None	12
Less than 1	1
From 1 to 20	1
From 20 to 100	—
(No answer, not applicable)	84

(e) For whom do you work?

	%
The government	1
A nationally owned private enterprise	3
A foreign-owned private enterprise	2
For myself	3
In an educational or research institution	7
Other (which): _____	
(No answer, not applicable)	84

8. What is your father's occupation? (If your father is not living, what was his occupation during the major part of his life? Please give details of his work, including his level of specialization and level of responsibility. Write freely in the space below. For example, "science teacher in public secondary school.")

(a) Write a brief description of his work, during an ordinary, typical workday.

(b) Does (or did) your father have subordinates, or people who work (or worked) under his direction? How many?

	%
None	69
Less than 1	21
11–20	4
20–100	4
More than 100	2

(c) For whom does he (or did he) work?

	%
The government	19
A nationally owned private enterprise	17
A foreign-owned private enterprise	7
For himself	36
In an educational or research institution	5
Other (which): ————————————	8
(No answer)	8

9. How many brothers and sisters do you have?

	Brothers %	Sisters %
None	26	29
One	34	32
Two	18	17
Three	11	9
Four	4	5
More than four	6	7
(No answer)	1	1

10. How many *older* brothers or sisters do you have?

	Brothers* %	Sisters %
None	57	60
One	24	20
Two	8	8
Three or more	10	10
(No answer)	—	2

11. With whom do you live and where?*

	%
With parents	56
With other relatives or older friends of your parents	7
In a boarding house for students	16
In a house or apartment with friend(s)	4
In a house or apartment alone	1
In a university dormitory or other university residence	5
With husband or wife	11
(No answer)	1

12. There is a lot of talk these days about social classes, and different people use different terms for referring to social classes. Below is a list of terms that are commonly used. Indicate which one you consider to be most applicable to your family (your parents), which one you consider to be most applicable to you ten years after completing your studies, and which one you consider most applicable to those who have completed their studies in your *facultad* (school or department).

	Your Family	Yourself, Ten Years after Graduation	The Majority of Those Who Have Graduated in Your *Facultad**
	%	%	%
Upper or wealthy class	3	10	7
Upper middle class	44	72	65
Lower middle class	33	14	21
Working class (*trabajadora*)	13	3	3
Poorer class (*obrera*)	4	—	—
Peasant class	1	—	—
(No answer)	1	2	5

13. What type of secondary school course did you have?**

	%
Scientific	91
Humanities	—
Industrial	—
Commercial	5
Agricultural	—
Other	12
(No answer)	1

14. During secondary school, in which subject did you do best, and
in which did you have the most difficulty?
(a) Your best subject: ————————————————
(b) Your worst subject: ————————————————

15. What type of student were you during secondary school?*

	%
Excellent	32
Good	53
Average	14
Poor	—
Very poor	—
(No answer)	—

16. In what year did you first enter the university?

	%
1964	11
1963	20
1962	19
1961	17
1960	10
1959	6
1955–1958	10
1954 or before	5

17. In what year of your university career are you enrolled?

	%
First	10
Second	23
Third	20
Fourth	21
Fifth	12
Sixth	9
Seventh	3
Eighth	1
(No answer)	1

18. In what *facultad* or school are you enrolled (for example: law,
medicine)? ————————————————

19. What is your specialization within your *facultad* (for example, in
engineering: civil engineering, electrical engineering)? ————

20. Have you changed your field of study since beginning your uni-

versity studies? (If you have changed more than once, note only the most recent change.)

	%
No	80
Yes, I previously studied ———————————	14
(No answer)	6

21. If you could begin your university studies over again, would you enroll in your present *facultad*?

	%
Yes	82
No	12
(No answer)	6

22. How important is it to you to complete your university studies?*

	%
Very important	90
Rather important	7
More or less important	2
Of little importance	—
(No answer)	—

23. If you could go to a foreign country to complete your studies or to do specialized studies, to what country would you most like to go?
Name of the country: —————————————————

24. Which of the following languages can you read? How easily can you read literature of your specialty in these languages? Please mark the number corresponding to the degree of difficulty that you have in reading these languages.

I can read:		Very Well	Fairly Well	With Some Diffi- culty	With Much Diffi- culty	I Cannot Read	(No Answer)
English	%	44	37	15	2	—	1
French	%	1	7	10	5	76	1
Another language (which):							
———————	%	1	5	5	2	87	1
(No answer)		—	—	—	—	—	—

25. When did you first consider seriously the career that you have chosen?

	%
Before primary school	2
During primary school	5
After finishing primary school and before beginning secondary school	6
During secondary school	25
After finishing secondary school and before entering university	20
After entering university	36
I have not yet decided on a career	5
(No answer)	1

26. Many factors influence the choice of a career. Which factors most influenced your career choice? Write your answer in the space provided below:

_____

_____

_____

27. In what occupation do you plan to work after graduating? Write in the name of the occupation and answer the additional questions about the occupational situation in which you expect to work.

Name of the occupation: ──────────────────

I plan to work:*	%
for the government	20
in a nationally owned private enterprise	14
in a foreign-owned private enterprise	6
for myself	21
in an educational or research institution	27
other (which): ──────────────────	2
(No answer)	9

28. How likely is it that you will work in this occupation after graduating?

	%
Very likely	70
Rather likely	25
Not very likely	2
(No answer)	3

29. Considering the average person graduated from your *facultad*, how much do you think he will earn five years after graduation? And how about the average graduate in engineering and law, how much do you think they will earn five years after graduation? (If your *facultad* is engineering or law, do not answer for that one, but only for "your *facultad*.")

	Your Facultad %	Engineering %	Law %
Less than double the minimum salary†	14	3	3
2 to 3 times the minimum	31	12	7
4 to 6 times the minimum	38	26	24
6 to 10 times the minimum	3	12	13
10 to 15 times the minimum	2	2	6
15 to 20 times the minimum	—	—	1
20 to 30 times the minimum	—	—	1
30 to 50 times the minimum	—	—	—
More than 50 times the minimum	—	—	—
(No answer, not applicable)	12	45	45

† [These terms to be translated into national currency. "Minimum salary" refers to a legally prescribed minimum for salaried or hourly employees or, if there is none, to a figure representing a comparable salary.]

30. How would you compare yourself with other students in your class (year) with respect to general academic performance? Would you say that you are in:

	%
The upper quarter of your class	22
The upper half of your class	60
The lower half of your class	12
The lowest quarter of your class	1
(No answer)	5

31. What was your average grade in secondary school and what is it

now in university? If you don't know the exact grade, make an approximation.

(a) In secondary school: ─────────────────────
(b) In university: ─────────────────────

32. Do you have any courses to make up (repeat)?

	%
No	71
Yes, one	16
Yes, two	9
Yes, three or more	3
(No answer)	1

33. How do you think your standard of living, five years after graduation, will compare with your family's present standard of living?

	%
I expect that mine will be:	
much higher	30
a little higher	49
more or less the same	16
a little lower	4
much lower	—
(No answer)	1

34. What do you think is the most important factor for success in this country?*

	%
Competence	76
Luck	2
Personal contacts or family situation	18
(No answer)	5

35. What quality among the following would you most prefer in a professor of your *facultad*?

	%
To be a good lecturer	89
To know his material well	8
To be a good researcher (investigator)	1
(No answer)	2

36. There are various opinions concerning the qualities necessary for success in various university careers.

(a) Considering a person who is very intelligent but not very studious, in which of the following two types of careers do you think he would have the most success?

	%
Law or philosophy	61
Engineering or physics	35
(No answer)	4

(b) Considering a person who is very studious but not very intelligent, in which type of career do you think he would be most successful?*

	%
Law or philosophy	48
Engineering or physics	48
(No answer)	3

37. Of the following, which is the more important function of the university?

	%
To provide a general education to students	37
To prepare students for professional life	61
(No answer)	2

38. How satisfied are you with your life as a student, including all aspects—professors, courses, facilities, examinations?*

	%
Very satisfied	11
Satisfied	64
Unsatisfied	20
Very unsatisfied	3
(No answer)	1

39. How would you evaluate your professors in general, taking into account their knowledge of material, lectures, assignments, examinations?

	%
The majority are excellent.	70
Few or none are excellent.	28
(No answer)	2

40. How desirable is it that professors in your *facultad* be active in politics?

	%
Very desirable	10
Desirable	41
Undesirable	38

Very undesirable   9
(No answer)   2

41. To what extent do you think of yourself as belonging to each of the following categories of persons? For example, do you think of yourself as an intellectual most of the time, often, rarely, or never?

		Most of the Time	Often	Rarely	Never	(No Answer)
An intellectual	%	8	30	28	14	20
A scientist	%	3	20	26	22	29
A professional	%	23	35	16	11	15

42. If you had to define yourself in these terms, would you say that you are more an intellectual, a scientist, or a professional? (Choose only one.)*

	%
Intellectual	27
Scientist	12
Professional	57
(No answer)	5

43. How often do you discuss the following topics with fellow students?

		Every Day	Every Two or Three Days	At Least Once a Week	Less than Once a Week, but at Least Once a Month	Less than Once a Month	(No Answer)
Personal problems	%	19	18	22	15	20	6
Academic and career problems	%	25	28	20	12	4	11
Art and literature	%	7	14	25	20	16	18
National politics	%	18	20	24	17	10	11
International politics*	%	15	18	24	17	13	12
Student politics in your *facultad* or school*	%	16	20	22	19	13	9

Student politics
in general   %   16   16   23   18   19   8

44. If you had to choose between being an academic person—for
    example, a professor or a researcher—and being a politician—
    for example, a deputy or a senator—which would you choose?

	%
Professor or researcher	75
Deputy or senator	24
(No answer)	1

45. There is talk of a proposal to organize university careers so that
    students would not choose their field of specialization (*facultad*)
    until their third year, taking courses in several fields during their
    first two years of study. Some favor this new proposal, and others
    prefer the present system. What is your opinion?

	%
Favorable to the proposal	45
Opposed to the proposal	54
(No answer)	1

46. In many Latin American universities there are differences of opin-
    ion concerning the role to be played by university student govern-
    ment. Which of the following alternatives do you prefer?

	%
University student government should express student views concerning national and international politics.	30
University student government should be concerned solely with student and academic affairs.	69
(No answer)	1

47. Do most of your friends belong to:

	%
Your *facultad*	39
Other *facultades*	37
or:	
Most of them are not university students	20
(No answer)	4

48. Which of the changes listed below would you like to have in your
    facultad? Indicate only the one which you consider most impor-
    tant.

	%
Improvement of recreational activities (sports, cultural activities)	5
Improvement of educational facilities (library, laboratory)	19
More courses oriented toward practical application	33
More freedom to teach *(libertad de cátedra)*	3
More student participation in *facultad* and university government	24
(No answer)	16

49. In general, do your friends agree with you on political issues?

	%
All agree	2
Most agree	79
Few agree	15
None agree	1
(No answer)	3

50. How active are you in university affairs? For example, did you vote in the last elections of your *facultad* or school? Have you attended a meeting of the student council in your *facultad* or of the university in the past six months?

   (a) Voted in the last election of school or *facultad*

	%
Yes	35
No	46
No student council in school	12
(No answer)	7

   (b) Attended a meeting of a student council*

	%
Yes	29
No	63
No student council in school	—
(No answer)	7

51. Some people believe that the decisions of university student leaders should not be influenced by their affiliations with political parties outside the university, while others believe that such influence is all right. What is your opinion?

                                                                    %

   It is all right for student leaders to

represent the interests and ideologies of
national poltical parties in student politics.   30
Student leaders should have nothing to do with
the interests and ideologies of national
political parties.   69
(No answer)   1

52. There are considerable differences of opinion among students concerning the kinds of problems that would justify the student strike as an expression of student sentiments. Without considering the particular content of problems that might be involved in a particular strike, what is your general opinion with respect to the use of the strike in the following types of problems:

			Strikes Are Justified	Strikes Are Not Justified	(No Answer)
(a)	University issues*	%	74	24	3
(b)	National or international political issues	%	37	54	9

53. With respect to your own experience, in how many strikes or demonstrations have you participated actively?*

	%
None	78
One	13
Two	3
Three	1
Four or more	3
(No answer)	1

54. Which of the following kinds of organizations do you belong to? (Indicate as many as apply).

			Yes	No	(No Answer)
(a)	National political party or organization	%	14	43	2
(b)	Student political party	%	5	47	48
(c)	Cultural organization (those concerned with presenting plays, concerts,				

art expositions, literary meetings)	%	17	41	42
(d) Religious association	%	35	32	33
(e) Social or sports organization (sports club that presents social events, dances, fiestas)	%	45	23	32
(f) Professional or scientific association (those concerned with the interests and problems of the members of a career or field of study)	%	16	35	48
(g) Other type (which):————	%	9	21	69

55. Do you now occupy, or have you occupied in the past year, a position of formal responsibility (elective or appointive position) within one or more student organizations?

	%
Yes	33
No	64
(No answer)	3

56. How much interest do you have in questions of student politics?*

	%
A lot	21
Some	43
Little	24
None	12
(No answer)	1

57. How much interest do you have in the next national elections?*

	%
A lot	71
Some	22
A little	4
None	2
(No answer)	—

58. Below you will find a list of the most important parties that have competed in or have been influential in national elections within the last ten years. Indicate which one of these you, your father

(or guardian), and your best friend most prefer. In case you consider none of these as preferable, indicate the one which you would prefer, in general.

	You %	Your Father %	Your Best Friend %
Partido Estadista (PER)	25	31	34
Partido Independentista (PIP)	23	8	20
Partido Popular (PPD)	46	55	38
Partido Acción Cristiana (PAC)	2	2	1
(No answer)	3	4	6

59. If you had to make a choice among the following three things, which do you think is most important for this country?*

	%
Political democracy	30
Economic development	22
Social and economic equality	18
Political status	27
(No answer)	4

60. What do you think about this country joining the Latin American Free Trade Association?

	%
Strongly favor	29
Favor	31
Oppose	4
Strongly oppose	35
(No answer)	1

61. There is a lot of talk today about agrarian reform. How do you feel about it with respect to this country?

(a) Are you for or against it?*

	%
For	7
Against	66
(No answer)	28

(b) If you are in favor of agrarian reform, which form of compensation to landowners do you consider adequate?

	%
None	4

Cash in full	17
Cash and bonds	37
Bonds	10
Other (which?) ——————————————————	3
(No answer)	29

(c) Assuming that agrarian reform is carried out, what type of land tenure do you favor?

	%
Small private plots	44
Cooperative farms (one large farm owned by a number of families)	25
State-owned farms	3
Other (which?) ——————————————————	4
(No answer)	24

62. What is your opinion concerning the Alliance for Progress as it affects *this* country? Would you say that it is:*

	%
Very beneficial	58
Moderately beneficial	31
Has no effect on the country	5
Somewhat harmful	4
Very harmful	2
(No answer)	1

63. The Cuban Revolution has aroused a great deal of interest. Some people approve of the changes that have taken place there and others do not. Speaking generally about the form of government, the economy, and other changes, what is your opinion of the Cuban Revolution?

	%
Very favorable	3
Favorable	7
Unfavorable	30
Very unfavorable	58
(No answer)	2

64. With which one of the following statements are you most in agreement?

	%
The government should not intervene in the economic life of the country, but should leave the economic affairs in the hands of private parties.	4

The government should not own economic
enterprises, but should control some
aspects of their conduct.   47
The government should control some aspects
of the conduct of enterprises and industries
and should own the basic industries.   46
The government should own all industries
and control economic life of the country.   2
(No answer)   1

65. With which of the following statements are you most in agreement?

	%
Foreign capital brings only benefits to the nation.	11
Foreign capital has more good than bad effects on the nation.	76
Foreign capital has more bad than good effects on the nation.	9
Foreign capital is harmful to the nation.	3
(No answer)	1

66. Which would be the best solution to political status question for Puerto Rico?

	%
Commonwealth (Free Associated State)	25
Statehood	40
Independence	23
Do not know	11
(No answer)	1

67. Below are the names of some national and foreign statesmen and politicians. Indicate the degree to which you are favorable or unfavorable to the ideas and actions of these men.

		Strongly Approve	Approve More than Disapprove	Disapprove More than Approve	Strongly Disapprove	(No Answer)
Fidel Castro	%	2	3	15	77	3
John F. Kennedy	%	73	24	2	—	1
Nasser	%	1	18	45	19	18
Khrushchev	%	1	4	36	54	5
La Muñoz Marín	%	31	45	16	5	3
Luis Ferre	%	10	30	37	17	6

G. Concepción
de Gracia   %   10   19   38   24   8

68. Among the following fields of intellectual specialization, how would you classify the relative development of France, the United States, the Soviet Union, and this country? (In each field, mark an ✕ for the country you consider the most developed.)

	Physics and Mathematics %	Philosophy and History %	Art and Literature %	Social Sciences %
Puerto Rico	1	5	7	35
France	1	53	63	6
USSR	25	4	3	6
USA	42	15	10	33
(No answer)	32	24	16	19

69. Now we would like to ask your opinion about specific aspects of various countries. Draw a circle around the name of the country that you think is highest in each of the following characteristics:

(a) standard of living*

	USSR	USA	France	Red China	Sweden	(No Answer)
%	1	85	1	1	8	3

(b) economic development*

	USSR	USA	France	Red China	Sweden	(No Answer)
%	5	82	2	1	4	7

(c) individual liberty

	USSR	USA	France	Red China	Sweden	(No Answer)
%	—	69	6	—	21	4

(d) equal distribution of wealth*

	USSR	USA	France	Red China	Sweden	(No Answer)
%	27	33	2	1	25	11

(e) all things considered, the country toward which you have the most favorable feelings

	USSR	USA	France	Red China	Sweden	(No Answer)
%	2	80	5	1	9	3

(f) all things considered, the country with the greatest future

	USSR	USA	France	Red China	Sweden	(No Answer)
%	8	76	3	2	6	5

70. Now some questions about statements that people often hear. Many persons are totally in accord with these expressions, others are somewhat in agreement, and others totally disagree. Indicate your own response to each of the following:

		Agree Strongly	Agree Some-what	Dis-agree Some-what	Dis-agree Strongly	(No (Answer)
(1)	In order to be happy, one should conduct himself as others wish, even if this means keeping his own ideas to himself. %	1	15	29	54	1
(2)	The son of a laboring man does not have a very good chance of entering the liberal professions.* %	2	10	20	68	1
(3)	The city is not a very friendly place; people can make friends only among others similar to themselves* %	5	20	39	36	1
(4)	When choosing a job, one should arrange to work near his parents, even if this means losing a good opportunity. %	1	8	27	63	1
(5)	People in a big city are cold and im-					

		%					
	personal; it is hard to make new friends.	%	8	27	31	33	1
(6)	Making plans only brings unhappiness, because the plans are hard to fulfill.	%	2	9	33	55	1
(7)	The saints intercede and and pray for us.*	%	21	27	15	33	3
(8)	If you have a chance to hire an assistant in your work, it is always better to hire a relative instead of a stranger.*	%	15	34	28	21	1
(9)	With things as they are today, an intelligent person ought to think only about the present, without worrying about what is going to happen tomorrow.	%	3	4	22	70	1
(10)	Religion impedes the progress of the country.	%	3	8	20	67	2
(11)	It makes little difference if people choose one or an-						

		%				
	other candidate for political office, because nothing or very little will change.	%	2	4	16	77	1
(12)	Human nature being what it is, there will always be wars and conflicts.*	%	27	42	20	11	1
(13)	There are two kinds of people in the world: the strong and the weak.	%	22	34	24	19	1
(14)	In spite of everything one hears, political corruption has decreased in this country in recent years.	%	17	42	24	15	2
(15)	The most important thing a child should learn is to obey his parents.*	%	34	40	16	7	2
(16)	The only way to understand our present confused world is to listen to the leaders and other trustworthy persons.	%	6	28	35	28	3

(17)	All religions should have the same rights before the law.*	%	69	23	3	4	2
(18)	In spite of everything, the majority of politicians are still honest.	%	4	35	44	14	3
(19)	Puerto Ricans can do any-thing better than a foreigner.*	%	13	29	32	25	2
(20)	People should devote them-selves to their friends and comrades and not pardon their enemies and ad-versaries.	%	11	18	36	33	2
(21)	The health of a Puerto Rican is of greater value than the life of a foreigner.	%	4	14	31	49	2
(22)	One should not talk to people who have ideas opposed to his own.*	%	1	2	14	82	2
(23)	Every politi-cian is a thief, and the ones who are not						

	will become thieves if they are elected to office.*	%	2	6	27	63	1
(24)	A person can have confidence in people only if he knows them well.	%	15	37	29	18	1
(25)	A person can be both a Communist and a good Catholic.	%	7	8	15	69	1
(26)	Science and religion have basically opposed ways of seeing the world; these ways are inherently irreconcilable.*	%	12	18	34	35	2
(27)	A rapid increase in economic development would require substantial limitations on individual freedom.*	%	4	19	37	36	3
(28)	A rapid increase in economic development would require a much stronger, national government						

than we now have.*	%	10	23	38	28	2

(29) Differences in income among the various occupations should be reduced.*   %   8   23   35   31   2

71. Many people say that some groups have too much power in this country and some have too little, but they often disagree on which groups have too much or too little. For each of the following groups of people in this country, please indicate whether they have more or less power than you think they should.

		Have More Power than They Should	Have Less Power than They Should	(No Answer)
The wealthy*	%	81	9	9
Large corporations	%	81	10	9
Jews	%	28	45	27
Labor unions	%	51	32	17
The Church	%	40	42	18

72. Compared with most other students in the university, would you say that your general political position is:

	%
Much more left than most students	5
More left than most students	15
About the same as most students	44
More right than most students	25
Much more right than most students	6
(No answer)	5

73. What is your religion? your father's? your mother's?

	Yourself %	Father %	Mother %
Baptist	3	3	3
Other Protestant sects	8	9	11
Jewish	1	—	1
Catholic, practicing	47	25	45
Catholic, but non-practicing	26	40	28
Spiritualist	1	2	3
Other	1	1	2

I have no religion, but I believe in God	8	15	3
Atheist or agnostic	4	1	1
(No answer)	1	4	3

74. Do you consider yourself:

	%
Very religious	8
Moderately religious	71
Slightly religious	14
Not religious at all	6
(No answer)	1

75. How often do you attend church, temple, or synagogue? and your father? and your mother?

	Yourself %	Father %	Mother %
Never	9	28	9
Almost never	12	21	15
Once a year or more often, but less than once a month	13	12	13
Once or twice a month	11	6	11
Once a week	43	17	30
More than once a week	11	8	17
(No answer)	1	8	5

76. Would you say that your religious sentiments have changed since entering the university?*

	%
No, I am just as religious as before.	66
I have never been religious.	2
Now I am more religious.	10
Now I am less religious.	21
(No answer)	2

77. Concerning divorce, with which of the following statements do you most agree?

	%
Divorce should be permitted for anyone who wishes it.	31
Divorce should be allowed only in special cases.	57
Divorce should not be permitted to anyone.	10
(No answer)	2

78. With regard to married women working outside the home, what is your opinion?*

	%
Fully approve	14
More in favor than opposed	33
More opposed than favorable	44
Fully oppose	8
(No answer)	2

79. In your own case, when you are married (or if you are already married), how important is it to you to remain faithful to your spouse?*

	%
Very important	73
Rather important	23
Of little importance	2
Not important	1
(No answer)	2

80. In your own case, would you say that it is difficult to remain faithful to your spouse (or that it will be difficult when you are married)?

	%
Very difficult	5
Rather difficult	6
Somewhat difficult	19
Not difficult at all	68
(No answer)	2

81. If you were to enter a game between two teams that had already begun playing (a soccer game, for example), in which of the following situations would you most prefer to play?*

	%
With a team that was ahead by a large margin	10
With a team that was ahead by a small margin	8
In a game in which both teams were tied	63
With a team that was behind by a small margin	13
With a team that was behind by a large margin	3
(No answer)	4

82. When you have a difficult problem of any kind to solve, do you prefer to solve it yourself, without the help of anyone else?*

	%
Always	18

Usually	69
Rarely	11
Never	1
(No answer)	2

83. In general, would you say that you are a person who is:*

	%
Very happy	32
Moderately happy	58
Somewhat happy	8
Unhappy	1
(No answer)	2

84. How much do you enjoy reading serious literature?

	%
A great deal	34
Moderately	44
Some, but not much	18
Not at all	2
(No answer)	2

85. How much do you enjoy listening to classical music?*

	%
A great deal	29
Moderately	37
Some, but not much	28
Not at all	5
(No answer)	2

86. Do you ever think about the problems of the country, analyzing them and elaborating plans in your imagination to resolve them?*

	%
Frequently	38
Sometimes	40
Seldom	17
Never	2
(No answer)	2

87. Would you say that during your childhood and adolescence you were generally:

	%
Very happy	43
Rather happy	43
Rather unhappy	11

Very unhappy	1
(No answer)	2

88. Have you ever found yourself daydreaming, imagining yourself in situations in which you played an important role?*

	%
Frequently	34
Fairly often	41
Rarely	20
Never	4
(No answer)	2

Now, some questions concerning your health during the past two years.

89. Have you been bothered by nausea or stomach pains?

	%
Frequently	4
Fairly often	12
Rarely	31
Never	51
(No answer)	2

90. Have you experienced headaches?*

	%
Frequently	12
Fairly often	24
Rarely	34
Never	27
(No answer)	2

91. Have you had feelings of dizziness?*

	%
Frequently	1
Fairly often	5
Rarely	19
Never	72
(No answer)	2

Finally, some questions concerning your mental health. Answer these with respect to the last two years:

92. Have you had difficulties getting to sleep, either because you were thinking about something or for other reasons?*

	%
Frequently	9
Fairly often	17

Rarely   37
Never   34
(No answer)   2

93. Do you chew your fingernails?

                                           %
Frequently   12
Fairly often   11
Rarely   17
Never   57
(No answer)   2

94. Do you have nightmares?

                                           %
Frequently   2
Fairly often   11
Rarely   42
Never   43
(No answer)   2

95. Do you have feelings of fear or anxiety at night, during sleep?*

                                           %
Frequently   2
Fairly often   8
Rarely   28
Never   61
(No answer)   2

96. Do your palms sweat?

                                           %
Frequently   13
Fairly often   17
Rarely   32
Never   36
(No answer)   2

97. Have you experienced cold perspiration?

                                           %
Frequently   2
Fairly often   16
Rarely   42
Never   38
(No answer)   2

98. Have you felt depressed and sad?*

	%
Frequently	9
Fairly often	41
Rarely	39
Never	10
(No answer)	2

99. In general, how would you rate your mental health, and that of your father and mother?

	You	Father	Mother
	%	%	%
Excellent	40	34	34
Good	48	43	45
Average	9	13	14
Poor	1	2	2
Very poor	—	1	1
(No answer)	2	6	5

MANY THANKS FOR YOUR KIND COOPERATION. IS THERE ANYTHING YOU WOULD LIKE TO ADD? PLEASE WRITE ANY COMMENTS ON THE FOLLOWING PAGE.

Bibliography

BOOKS

Almand, Gabriel, and Sidney Verba. *Civic Culture.* Boston: Little, Brown and Company, 1965.

Anderson, Robert. *Party Politics in Puerto Rico.* Stanford: Stanford University Press, 1965.

Benítez, Jaime. *La casa de estudios.* San Juan, P.R.: Editorial Universitaria, 1956.

Benjamin, Harold R. W. *Higher Education in the American Republics.* New York: McGraw-Hill Book Company, 1965.

Berbusse, Edward J., S. J. *The United States in Puerto Rico, 1898–1900.* Chapel Hill: University of North Carolina Press, 1966.

Brameld, Theodore. *The Remaking of a Culture.* New York: Harper and Row, Publishers, 1959.

Bereday, George Z. F., and J. A. Lauwerys (eds.). *Higher Education: The Yearbook of Education, 1959.* Yonkers on Hudson, N.Y.: World Book Company, 1959.

Campbell, Angus; Philip Converse; Warren Miller; and Donald Stokes. *The American Voter.* New York: John Wiley and Sons, Inc., 1964.

Clark, Victor S. *Porto Rico and Its Problems.* Washington, D. C.: The Brookings Institution, 1930.

Coleman, James S. (ed.). *Education and Political Development.* Princeton: Princeton University Press, 1965.

Columbia University, Teachers College. *A Survey of the Public Educational System of Puerto Rico.* New York: Bureau of Publications, Teachers College, Columbia University, 1926.

De Vries, Egbert, and José Medina Echavarría (eds.). *Social Aspects of Economic Development in Latin America.* Vol. 1. Paris: UNESCO, 1963.

Echavarría, José Medina, and Benjamin Higgins (eds.). *Social Aspects of Economic Development in Latin America.* Vol. 2. Paris: UNESCO, 1963.

Falcón, Luis Nieves. *Recruitment to Higher Education in Puerto Rico, 1940–1960*. Río Piedras: Editorial Universitaria, 1965.

Feuer, Lewis. *The Conflict of Generations*. New York: Basic Books, Inc., Publishers, 1968.

Glazer, Nathan, and Daniel P. Moynihan. *Beyond the Melting Pot: The Ethnic Groups of New York City*. Cambridge, Massachusetts: The M. I. T. Press, 1963.

Glock, Charles Y., and Rodney Stark. *Religion and Society in Tension*. Chicago: Rand McNally and Company, 1965.

Goldsen, Rose K.; Morris Rosenberg; Rubin Williams, Jr.; and Edward Suchman. *What College Students Think*. Princeton: Van Nostrand Co., Inc., 1960.

Harbison, Frederick, and Charles A. Myers (eds.). *Manpower and Education*. New York: McGraw-Hill Book Company, 1965.

Hartz, Louis (ed.). *The Foundation of New Societies*. New York: Harcourt, Brace and World, Inc., 1964.

Harris, Seymour E. (ed.). *Higher Education in the United States*. Cambridge, Mass.: Harvard University Press, 1960.

Hyman, Herbert. *Political Socialization*. Glencoe, Ill.: The Free Press, 1959.

Jacob, Philip E. *Changing Values in College*. New York: Harper and Row, Publishers, 1958.

Johnson, John J. (ed.). *Continuity and Change in Latin America*. Stanford: Stanford University Press, 1964.

Kautsky, John H. (ed.). *Political Change in Underdeveloped Countries: Nationalism and Communism*. New York: John Wiley and Sons, Inc., 1962.

Landy, David. *Tropical Childhood*. Chapel Hill: University of North Carolina Press, 1956.

Lane, Robert. *Political Life*. Glencoe, Ill.: The Free Press, 1959.

Lazarsfeld, Paul F.; Bernard Berelson; and Harold Gaudet. *The People's Choice*. New York: Columbia University Press, 1948.

Lazarsfeld, Paul F., and Wagner Thielens, Jr. *The Academic Mind: Social Scientists in Time of Crisis*. Glencoe, Ill.: The Free Press, 1958.

Lenski, Gerhard. *The Religious Factor*. Garden City, N.Y.: Doubleday and Company, Inc., 1963.

Lewis, Gordon K. *Puerto Rico: Freedom and Power in the Caribbean*. New York: Monthly Review Press, 1963.

Lipset, Seymour M. *First New Nation*. New York: Basic Books, Inc., Publishers, 1963.

————. *Political Man: The Social Bases of Politics*. Garden City, N.Y.: Anchor Books, Doubleday and Company, Inc., 1963.

Lipset, Seymour M.; Martin Trow; and James Coleman. *Union Democracy*. Glencoe, Ill.: The Free Press, 1956.

Lipset, Seymour M., and Sheldon S. Wolin (eds.). *The Berkeley Student Revolt: Facts and Interpretations*. Garden City, N.Y.: Doubleday and Company, Inc., 1965.

Morales-Carrión, Arturo. *Puerto Rico and the Non-Hispanic Caribbean: A Study in the Decline of Spanish Exclusivism*. San Juan, P.R.: Editorial Universitaria, 1952.

National Catholic Almanac, 1965. Garden City, N.Y.: Doubleday and Company, Inc., 1965.

Newcombe, Theodore M. *Personality and Social Change*. New York: Holt, Rinehart and Winston, 1943.

Newcombe, Theodore M., and Everett K. Wilson (eds.). *College Peer Groups*. Chicago: Aldine Publishing Company, 1966.

Osuna, Juan José. *A History of Education in Puerto Rico*. Río Piedras, P.R.: Ediciones de la Universidad de Puerto Rico, 1949.

Petrullo, Vincenzo. *Puerto Rican Paradox*. Philadelphia: University of Pennsylvania Press, 1947.

Polsby, Nelson W.; Robert A. Dentler; and Paul A. Smith (eds.). *Politics in Social Life*. Boston: Houghton Mifflin Company, 1963.

Reynolds, Lloyd G., and Peter Gregory. *Wages, Productivity, and Industrialization in Puerto Rico*. Homewood, Ill.: Richard D. Irwin, Inc., 1965.

Sanford, Nevitt (ed.). *The American College*. New York: John Wiley and Sons, Inc., 1962.

Steward, Julian H.; Robert Manners; Eric K. Wolf; Ellen Padilla Seda; Sidney Mintz; and Raymond Scheele. *The People of Puerto Rico*. Champagne-Urbana: University of Illinois Press, 1956.

Stouffer, Samuel A. *Communism, Conformity, and Civil Liberties*. Garden City, N.Y.: Doubleday and Company, Inc., 1955.

Stycos, J. Mayone. *Family and Fertility in Puerto Rico*. New York: Columbia University Press, 1955.

Trotsky, Leon. *The History of the Russian Revolution*. Ann Arbor: The University of Michigan Press, 1932.

Tugwell, Rexford G. *The Stricken Land*. Garden City, N.Y.: Doubleday and Company, Inc., 1947.

Tumin, Melvin, with Arnold Feldman. *Social Class and Social Change in Puerto Rico*. Princeton: Princeton University Press, 1961.

Weiner, Myron. *The Politics of Scarcity: Public Pressure and Political Response in India*. Chicago: University of Chicago Press, 1962.

Williamson, Robert C. *El estudiante colombiano y sus actitudes.* Bogotá: Facultad de Sociologia, Universidad Nacional de Colombia, 1962.

ARTICLES AND PERIODICALS

Alderice, Jane. "The Case for Private School," *San Juan Review* 2 (June, 1965): 46–48.

Bachrach, Peter. "Attitude toward Authority and Party Preference in Puerto Rico," *Public Opinion Quarterly* 22 (1958): 68–73.

Bakke, E. Wight. "Students on the March: The Cases of Mexico and Colombia," *Sociology of Education* 37 (Spring, 1964): 200–228.

Denis, Manuel Maldonado. "Política y cultura puertorriqueña," *Revista de Ciencias Sociales* 7 (March and June, 1963): 141–148.

Edelstein, Alex A. "Since Bennington: Evidence of Change in Student Political Behavior," *Public Opinion Quarterly* 26 (Winter, 1962): 564–577.

Fischer, Joseph. "The University Student in South and Southeast Asia," *Minerva* 2 (Autumn, 1963).

Hull, Adrian. "The English Problem," *San Juan Review* 2 (June, 1965).

El Imparcial, May–July, 1965.

Lipset, Seymour M. "University Students and Politics in Underdeveloped Countries," *Minerva* 3 (Autumn, 1963).

Marques, René. "El puertorriqueño dócil," *Revista de Ciencias Sociales* 7 (March and June, 1963): 35–78.

Morse, Richard M. "La transformación ilusoria de Puerto Rico," *Revista de Ciencias Sociales* 4 (June, 1960): 357–376.

El Mundo, October 28–30, 1964, and May–July, 1965.

New York Times, November 9, 1946; December 18, 1947; April 16, 1948; May 9, 1948; October 29–30, 1964; March 6, 1966.

Nogee, Phillip, and Marvin B. Levin. "Some Determinants of Political Attitudes among College Voters," *Public Opinion Quarterly* 22 (Winter, 1958): 449–463.

"*San Juan Review* Interviews the Secretary of Education," *San Juan Review* 2 (June, 1965).

San Juan Star, October 29, 1964; October 30, 1964; May–July, 1965; July 7, 1965.

Selvin, Hannan, and Warren O. Hagstrom. "Determinants of Support for Civil Liberties," *British Journal of Sociology* 11 (March, 1960): 51–73.

Shimbori Michiya. "Zengakureu: A Japanese Case Study of a Student Political Movement," *Sociology of Education* 37 (Spring, 1964).

Time, September 9, 1966.

Torres, José Arsenio. "UPR: Will It Get Worse?" *San Juan Review* 2 (June, 1965).

Wagenheim, Kal. "Education in Puerto Rico," *San Juan Review* 2 (June, 1965).

———. "Puerto Rico: Kinship or Colony," *New Leader* 49 (May 23, 1966).

Walker, Kenneth N. "Determinants of Castro Support among Latin American University Students," reprinted from *Social and Economic Studies* 14 (March, 1965): 88–105.

Washington, Walter S. "Student Politics in Latin America: The Venezuelan Example," *Foreign Affairs* 37 (1959), 463–473.

GOVERNMENT BULLETINS, REPORTS, AND UNPUBLISHED MATERIAL

Bonilla, Frank. "Students in Politics: Three Generations of Political Action in a Latin American University." Ph.D. dissertation, Harvard University, 1959.

Carroll, Henry K. *Report on the Island of Porto Rico.* Washington, D. C.: U. S. Government Printing Office, 1899.

Carson, Arthur. *Higher Education in the Philippines.* U. S. Department of Health, Education, and Welfare, Office of Education, Bulletin 1961, no. 29. Washington, D. C.: U. S. Government Printing Office, 1961.

Center of Latin American Studies. *Statistical Abstract of Latin America, 1963.* University of California, Los Angeles, 1963.

Consejo Superior de Enseñanza. *Podrá mi hijo ingresar en la universidad.* Río Piedras, P. R.: Universidad de Puerto Rico, n.d.

Comparative National Development Project. "Colombia." Mimeographed. University of California, Berkeley: Institute of International Studies, 1965.

———. "Mexico." Mimeographed. University of California, Berkeley: Institute of International Studies, 1965.

———. "Puerto Rico." Mimeographed. University of California, Berkeley: Institute of International Studies, March, 1965.

Curtis, Thomas D. *Land Reform, Democracy, and Economic Interest in Puerto Rico.* Tucson: University of Arizona, Division of Economic and Business Research, College of Business and Public Administration, November, 1966.

Department of Public Education, Puerto Rico. "Poder de retención de las escuelas de Puerto Rico." Mimeographed. September 27, 1961.

The Executive Committee of FUPI (ed.). "¿Qués es la FUPI?" Mimeographed. Río Piedras, P. R., 1963.

Faust, August F. *Brazil: Education in an Expanding Economy.* Washington, D. C.: U. S. Government Printing Office, 1960.

Frieburger, Adela R., and Charles Hauch. *Education in Chile.* Studies in Comparative Education Series. Washington, D. C.: U. S. Government Printing Office, 1963.

———. *Ecuador, Educational Data.* Education around the World Series. Washington, D. C.: U. S. Government Printing Office, 1962.

Frieburger, Adela R., and L. B. Watt. *Latin America.* Washington, D. C.: U. S. Government Printing Office, 1961.

Glazer, Myron. "The Professional and Political Attitudes of Chilean University Students." Ph.D. dissertation, Princeton University, 1965.

Hauch, Charles C. *The Current Situation in Latin American Education.* Washington, D. C.: Health, Education and Welfare Bulletin 1963, no. 21, U. S. Government Printing Office, 1962.

Heist, Paul. "Intellect and Commitment: The Faces of Discontent." Mimeographed. University of California, Berkeley: Center for the Study of Higher Education, 1966.

Johnston, Marjorie C. *Education in Mexico.* Washington, D. C.: U. S. Government Printing Office, 1956.

Junta de Plantificación. *Indicadores económicos de Puerto Rico.* San Juan: Estado Libre Asociado de Puerto Rico, 1965.

———. *Informe Económico al Gubernador,* 1964. San Juan: Estado Libre Asociado de Puerto Rico, 1965.

King, Margaret L., and George A. Male. *Spain, Educational Data.* Education around the World Series. Washington, D. C.: U. S. Government Printing Office, 1959.

Krumiviede, Grace I., and Charles C. Hauch. *Argentina, Educational Data.* Education around the World Series. Washington, D. C.: U. S. Government Printing Office, 1961.

———. *Bolivia, Educational Data.* Education around the World Series. Washington, D. C.: U. S. Government Printing Office, 1961.

Male, George. *Education in the Republic of Haiti.* Washington, D. C.: U. S. Government Printing Office, 1959.

Newcombe, Theodore M., and K. A. Feldman. "The Impacts of Colleges upon Their Students." A report to the Carnegie Foundation for the Advancement of Teaching, January, 1968.

Office of Education, U. S. Department of Health, Education and Welfare. *The Current Situation in Latin American Education.* Washington, D. C.: U. S. Government Printing Office, 1963.

———. *Digest of Educational Statistics, 1965.* Washington, D. C.: U. S. Government Printing Office, 1965.

———. *Opening (Fall) Enrollment in Higher Education, 1964.* Washington, D. C.: U. S. Government Printing Office, 1964.

Sánchez, George I. *Development of Education in Venezuela.* Washington, D. C.: U. S. Government Printing Office, 1963.

Sussman, Leila. "High School to University in Puerto Rico." Mimeographed. Social Science Research Center, University of Puerto Rico, 1965.

Thompson, M. Weldon. *Education in Honduras.* Washington, D. C.: U. S. Government Printing Office, 1961.

UNESCO. *Basic Facts and Figures: International Statistics Relating to Education, Culture and Mass Communication.* Paris, 1961.

U. S. Bureau of Census. *U. S. Census of Population: 1960.* Vol. 1. Washington, D. C.: U. S. Government Printing Office, 1963.

————. *Statistical Abstracts of the United States, 1964.* Washington, D. C.: U. S. Government Printing Office, 1964.

University Bulletin of General Information, 1964–65. Río Piedras, University of Puerto Rico, 1963.

University of Puerto Rico. *Ley universitaria y reglamentos.* Edición revisada. San Juan, P. R.: Editorial Universitaria, 1962.

Index

Index 203

Japan: student political activity in, 114
junior colleges: pressure for, 39

Kennedy, John F.: 178
Krushchev, Nikita: 178

land law: 111
Lares: revolt of 1868 in, 5
Latin American Free Trade Association: student attitude toward, 176
Left, the. SEE Proindependence Movement; University Federation for Independence
London School of Economics: 128

manufacturing: growth of, 19, 20
Mao Tse-tung: 133, 134
Maris Bras, Juan: 141
Marques, René: 111
Marx, Karl: 4, 139
mass media: U.S. orientation of, 15, 18; and Latin America, 16; and status issue, 29; and FUPI, 132; on campus disturbances, 141; radicalization of Puerto Ricans by, 152
Mexico: secondary education in, 38; education of women in, 45; student political activity in, 114. SEE ALSO National University of Mexico.
Mayagüez (P.R.): 141
Meyerson, Martin: 129
MPI. SEE Proindependence Movement
El Mundo: 141
Muñoz Marín, Luis: and PPD reform, 25; mentioned, 18, 143, 178

Nassar, Gamal Abdul: 174
nationalism: under Spain, 4–5, 10–11; under U.S., 6; and education abroad, 9, 10; and Puerto Rican history, 10, 112; and economy, 30, 147, 148, 149; in FUPI, 130, 134, 143–144, 147; student support for, 148. SEE ALSO Nationalist party; Proindependence Movement; University Federation for Independence
Nationalist party: defeated in 1932, 6; assassination by, 6; revolt of in 1950, 6; at University of Puerto Rico, 92, 93

national politics: student interest in, 106, 175. SEE ALSO University Federation for Independence
National University, Colombia: women's conservatism at, 63; and leftism, 90–91; political orientation of schools at, 100–101
National University of Mexico: political orientation of schools at, 101
NATO: 133
Nicaragua: 45

PAC. SEE Christian Action party
PER. SEE Republican Statehood party
Philippines, the: 50, 98
PIP. SEE Puerto Rican Independent party
Popular Democratic party (Partido Popular Democrático): and economy, 18, 19, 25–26; election record of, 24, 26 Table 1, 74; social program of, 25–26; and status issue, 25, 59; general support for, 26; student support for, 30, 31, 53–62 passim, 69–70, 99, 104, 116, 121, 146; split of, 149, 151; mentioned, 16, 112, 143
Populares. SEE Popular Democratic party
PPD. SEE Popular Democratic party
Proindependence Movement (Movimento Pro-Independencia): opposed to U.S., 28; and Castro, 28; general support for, 28–29; and FUPI, 131, 142; and 1964 boycott, 140, 141; mentioned, 147
Protestant churches: and lower classes, 73–74
Puerto Rican Independent party (Partido Independentista Puertorriqueño): election record of, 6, 26 Table 1, 27; as official left, 27; and status issue, 27–28; general support for, 28; student support for, 30–31, 53–62 passim, 64, 69–70, 80, 83, 86, 104, 108, 116–121 passim, 121, 146; formation of, 59
Puerto Rico: as Spanish colony, 4–5, 7–11 passim; as U.S. commonwealth, 22, 24. SEE ALSO culture; economy; education; nationalism
Puerto Rico Industrial Development Corporation. SEE Fomento